NO
PROJECT MANAGEMENT
BY POWERPOINT

Observations and Advice on Better Project Execution
in the Financial Services Industry

TODD B. LOEB, PMP

ISBN-10: 0615791719
ISBN-13: 978-0615791715

Library of Congress Control Number: 2013906008
The Mascar Group Hingham,
Massachusetts

DEDICATION

This book is dedicated to Marta, Max and Oscar – my family...my everything... without whom I would have and be nothing...

It is also dedicated to the memory of my friend Ron Olmstead, who shaped my career more than he probably ever knew...

CONTENTS

PREFACE

This book had to be written. It had to be written simply because the subject matter—project management in financial services—had strangely never been covered extensively unto itself in lengthy literary fashion. Sure, there are countless books on project management—and probably the same number of tomes examining the various aspects of the financial services industry. Yet the specific and unique way that financial services projects must be addressed and delivered hardly ever—if at all—warranted the publishing of a full-blown book. That is, until now.

Having spent the last twenty-five years in the financial services sector, I have seen project management evolve from something the techie people did to track their hours to cloud-enabled collaborative apps that synch with mobile devices in real time. I have watched the Project Management Professional (PMP) designation—one I have held for ten years—go from a "what does that stand for" to an absolutely "must have" requirement for applying to many industry project management jobs. I have seen project management consulting explode in growth, contract to nearly non-existence, then grow again. Yet through all of this, very few people thought the examination of project management in financial services worthy of a detailed examination.

That is, until now.

INTRODUCTION

No Project Management by PowerPoint examines the practices, processes, tools, and future of project management in the financial services industry. Through example and observation, this book takes a detailed look at the unique attributes of financial projects and how the people charged with delivering these initiatives might best achieve success.

No Project Management by PowerPoint is both a review of the current environment of financial services project management and a helpful guide to improving the way you execute your day-to-day PM responsibilities. Within these pages, you will explore such topics as project and role definitions, the various methods of defining success, and how financial projects are managed along traditional or non-traditional paths. The book also examines the project manager in the industry—how they may assume the role of project manager, the multitude of career options, and what the future may hold professionally for Financial Services Project Managers.

Beyond these definitions, frameworks, and organizational analysis, this book presents a very pragmatic—and often tongue in cheek—view of financial services project management. Each chapter contains either a real-world tip, war story, or sage piece of advice from experienced industry practitioners. Whether it's showing a way of creating an ad-hoc work breakdown structure or recommending a simple presentation idea on how to quickly and simply set stakeholder expectations.

No Project Management by PowerPoint is more than a book on project management—it's a practitioner's guide to improving how we, as financial services professionals, manage the daily demands of our projects, our industry, and our own careers.

CHAPTER 1:
A Brief Look at the Financial Services Industry

The financial services industry has gone through dramatic change over the last few years. From the run-up of the financial markets in the early 2000s through the financial crisis of 2008, and now with our burgeoning "recovery," the industrial sector we call finance has seen growth, contraction, then growth again in a way that not only has had an effect on those who work within it, but on society itself. Very few of us went untouched by what happened there over the last few years. Many of us remain either its victim or its beneficiary.

Yet for those of us who have spent their project management careers toiling in and about financial services, the last five or so years truly has been both the infamous "blessing and a curse." The "curse," of course, for the obvious reason that remaining gainfully (or even *not* gainfully) employed has been a challenge. We all know that the unemployment rate in the US went from 4.6 percent in January of 2007 to 9.8 percent in March in 2010.[1] In the financial services sector specifically, our own unemployment rate went from 1.9 percent to over 7.8 percent[2] over the same period. Pretty scary stuff.

The financial crisis does, however, also have the potential to become a project management employment blessing. All of the industry projects that *did not* get done during

---

[1] U.S. Department of Labor, Bureau of Labor Statistics (2012)

[2] U.S. Department of Labor, Bureau of Labor Statistics (2012)

the worst times of the crisis have created an incredible backlog of work that eventually will need to *get* done. This queue includes both basic systems and maintenance projects—the "keeping the lights on" work—that could not be funded, as well as any *new* business ideas that could not get started during the difficult times. Also waiting in line are the myriad of projects spawned from the industry regulations created by governing bodies to ensure that the type of financial crisis that occurred in 2008 does not happen again. Compliance projects; reporting projects; new accounting systems that need to be developed; support organizations that need to be defined; older, legacy systems that need to be updated or totally replaced to meet new regulations—all have the potential for creating a robust economy for industry professionals focused on managing and delivering projects. As a matter of fact, the Financial Services industry spent over $350 billion in IT projects alone in 2009. That number increased to $373 billion in 2011.[3] By subsector, the insurance industry contributed $97.9 billion and the securities sector $75.2 billion, while banking spent $169.6 million of the total for 2011.[4] As mentioned above, compliance and risk management systems will make up a great deal of this work. A new report from IDC Financial Insights found that risk technology spending worldwide across the banking, capital markets, and insurance sectors will reach over $74 billion by 2015. Growth in IT spending on risk management will top 15 percent of total IT spending in financial services in 2012, according to IDC.[5]

So with this as a backdrop, let's take a few moments to define the financial services industry. The information provider ***Hoover's*** describes the financial services industry as "providing products and services to facilitate the flow of money." The would include banks, investment banks, consumer and commercial lenders, asset managers, brokerages, stock exchanges, payment processors, collection agencies, and private equity and venture capital investors. Also included would be the insurance field—organizations that provide life insurance, property and casualty insurance, health insurance, surety insurance, title insurance, credit insurance, and mortgage insurance. Companies that provide reinsurance coverage, insurance and reinsurance brokerage services, and risk management services are included here as well. Let's take a quick look at a few examples of these organizations and what they do.[6]

Investment Banks—Investment banking technically refers to the area of corporate finance that helps large, institutional clients raise funds (by issuing securities for either

---

[3] *IT Spending in Financial Services: A Global Perspective,* Celent by Jacob Jegher, January 26, 2011

[4] *IT Spending in Financial Services: A Global Perspective,* Celent - by Jacob Jegher, January 26, 2011

[5] *IT Risk Spending In Financial Services To Reach $74 Billion Worldwide by 2015,* Wallstreetandtechnology.com

[6] Information provided by Wikinvest.com

equity or debt) and advises clients during mergers, acquisitions, and other financial transactions. Most of the firms considered to be leaders in this sector, however, are not pure investment banks in this technical sense. The line between investment banks and commercial banks has become blurred, with each dabbling in the other's traditional territory. Though investment banks have become increasingly diversified, they are still commonly referred to simply as "investment banks." Good examples of this type of firm would be Goldman Sachs, Bank of America, Merrill Lynch, and JP Morgan. It is interesting to note that during the financial crisis of 2008, several of the organizations known as "traditional" investment banks chose to abandon that status converting themselves into "traditional bank holding companies," thereby making themselves eligible[7] to receive billions of dollars each in emergency taxpayer-funded assistance.[8] By making this change, referred to as a technicality, banks would be more tightly regulated. These banks received part of a $700 billion Troubled Asset Relief Program (TARP) intended to stabilize the economy and thaw the frozen credit markets.[9] Eventually, taxpayer assistance to banks reached nearly $13 trillion, most without much scrutiny;[10] lending did not increase[11] and credit markets remained frozen.[12]

Commercial Banks—Commercial banking includes firms that take deposits and make loans to customers, both corporate and individual. These companies offer much more than just checking accounts and auto loans, but the fact that they deal with the storage and lending of money is the basic factor that distinguishes them from other financial institutions. Examples of such firms would be Wachovia and Wells Fargo.

Money Center Banks—Money center banks are massive firms that operate in several different areas of the financial services industry. Essentially commercial banks, these are the firms that have delved into investment banking, asset management, etc., in an attempt to become "one-stop shops" for their customers. This seems to have worked,

---

[7] Jagger, Suzy "End of the Wall Street investment bank." The Times (London) (September 22, 2008).. Retrieved March 7, 2011.

[8] Matt Taibbi, "The Great American Bubble Machine." Rolling Stone magazine (April 5, 2010). Retrieved March 7, 2011.

[9] Erin Nothwehrm. "Emergency Economic Stabilization Act of 2008," University of Iowa (December 2008). Retrieved March 7, 2011.

[10] "The true cost of the bank bailout" PBS/WNET "Need to Know" (September 3, 2010). Retrieved March 7, 2011.

[11] Samuel Sherraden, "Banks use TARP funds to boost lending – NOT!" The Washington Note (July 20, 2009). Retrieved March 7, 2011.

[12] "Fed May Keep Rates Low as Tight Credit Impedes Small Businesses" Bloomberg BusinessWeek (April 26, 2010). Retrieved March 7, 2011.

as these companies are among the largest in the world, and include Citigroup, Bank of America, and Barclay's

Retail Banking—This is your typical mass-market bank in which individual customers use local branches of larger commercial banks. Services offered include savings and checking accounts, mortgages, personal loans, debit/credit cards, and certificates of deposit (CDs). Examples of retail banks would be Sovereign Bank or Eastern Bank.

Mutual Fund Companies[13]—A mutual fund is a type of investment company that pools money from many investors and invests the money in stocks, bonds, money-market instruments, other securities, or even cash. Here are some characteristics of mutual funds:

- Investors purchase shares in the mutual fund from the fund itself, or through a broker for the fund, and cannot purchase the shares from other investors on a secondary market, such as the New York Stock Exchange or NASDAQ stock market. The price that investors pay for mutual fund shares is the fund's approximate net asset value (NAV) per share plus any fees that the fund may charge at purchase, such as sales charges (also known as sales loads).
- Mutual fund shares are "redeemable." This means that when mutual fund investors want to sell their fund shares, they sell them back to the fund, or to a broker acting for the fund, at their current NAV per share, minus any fees the fund may charge, such as deferred sales loads or redemption fees.
- Mutual funds generally sell their shares on a continuous basis, although some funds will stop selling when, for example, they reach a certain level of assets under management.
- The investment portfolios of mutual funds typically are managed by separate entities known as "investment advisers" that are registered with the SEC. In addition, mutual funds themselves are registered with the SEC and subject to SEC regulation.

Brokerage—A brokerage is a licensed firm or an individual (known as a broker) that buys and sells stocks for its clients. There are several types of brokerage; the choice of brokerage depends upon how involved the individual investor wants to be.

- Full-service brokerage—provides research and advice to clients and sometimes, financial planning. This type of brokerage works for the investor with little or

---

[13] U.S Securities and Exchange Commission. http://www.sec.gov/answers/mutfund.htm

no inclination to spend time researching stocks. An example of a full-service brokerage is Salomon Smith Barney.

- Discount brokerage—provides fewer services and has lower commission rates. With this type of brokerage, the client does more of the work. An example of a discount brokerage is Charles Schwab.
- Deep discount brokerage—usually only executes trades and offers no or very few other services. The individual investor is the most involved with this type of brokerage. An example of a deep discount brokerage is Scottrade.

Custodian Bank—A Custodian bank, or simply a custodian, is a specialized financial institution responsible for safeguarding a firm's or individual's financial assets and is not likely to engage in "traditional" commercial or consumer/retail banking such as mortgage or personal lending, branch banking, personal accounts, ATMs and so forth. The role of a custodian in such a case would be to:

- hold in safekeeping assets/securities such as stocks, bonds, commodities like precious metals, and currency (cash), domestic and foreign
- arrange settlement of any purchases and sales and deliveries in/out of such securities and currency
- collect information on and income from such assets (dividends in the case of stocks/equities and coupons (interest payments) in the case of bonds) and administer related tax withholding documents and foreign tax reclamation;
- administer voluntary and involuntary corporate actions on securities held such as stock dividends, splits, business combinations (mergers), tender offers, or bond calls
- provide information on the securities and their issuers such as annual general meetings and related proxies
- maintain currency/cash bank accounts, effect deposits and withdrawals, and manage other cash transactions
- perform foreign exchange transactions
- often perform additional services for particular clients such as mutual funds; examples include fund accounting, administration, legal, compliance, and tax support services
- provide regular and special reporting on any or all their activities to their clients or authorized third parties.

Custodian banks are often referred to as global custodians if they safekeep assets for their clients in multiple jurisdictions around the world, using their own local branches or other local custodian banks with which they contract to be in their "global network" in each market to hold accounts for their respective clients.

Looking at the size of the financial services market, the wealth generated by the financial services industry contributes nearly 6 percent to US GDP[14], and is the largest US equity market sector, accounting for 20 percent of the market capitalization of the S&P 500 in the United States. In nearly half the country, the industry provides for 6 percent or more of *state* gross domestic product. In traditional financial hubs such as New York and Massachusetts, the industry accounted for 16.4 percent and 9.7 percent of overall state GDP, respectively, in 2008. The sector also supports a significant number of jobs and tax revenue in states such as Illinois, Pennsylvania, Texas, Florida, Connecticut, Georgia, South Dakota, and Delaware, where the industry directly employs at least 20,000 individuals in each state.[15]

As mentioned above, the financial services industry is a very large employer in the United States. Financial services positions make up about 6 percent of the overall jobs in the services sector of U.S. employment.[16] The services sector is probably the most vibrant and fastest growing component of the U.S. economy today, accounting for more than 78 percent of US Gross Domestic Product (GDP) in 2009, according to the U.S. Department of Commerce, Bureau of Labor Statistics (BLS), 'Employment by Sector,' November 2009. The same BLS report showed that during the period 1998–2008, services industries added about 14 million jobs, in contrast to the loss of over 2.9 million jobs in goods-producing industries. BLS also predicted future job growth to match this trend, with a 14.6 million increase in employment projected for 2008–2018, and with service industries accounting for almost all of the job growth.

Specifically, there are 7,724,000[17] people employed in the financial services industry in the United States. That is almost a 2 percent *decrease* from 2002. By the year 2020, there will be approximately 8,410,000 working in our industry, a 1 percent annual increase from 2010.[18]

---

[14] U.S. Financial Services Industry—Securities Industry and Financial Markets Association 2010

[15] Bureau of Economic Analysis and Commerce. "Significant" is defined as more than 5 percent of overall GDP per state.

[16] United States Department of Labor Bureau of Labor Statistics (2012)

[17] United States Department of Labor Bureau of Labor Statistics (2012)

[18] United States Department of Labor Bureau of Labor Statistics (2012)

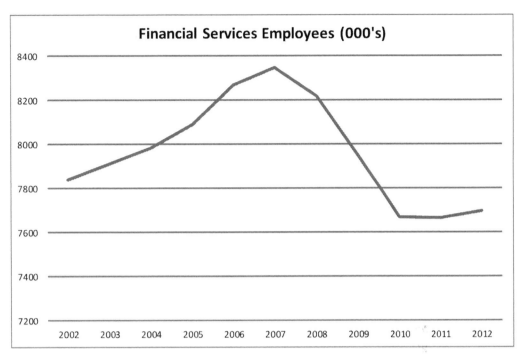

United States Department of Labor Bureau of Labor Statistics (2012)

So what does all of this mean for project managers and the people that work on projects? It means that the potential exists for long-term gainful employment. I say the *potential*, because being a successful project manager in the financial services space takes a lot more than desire and a PMP certification. Being a successful project manager in financial services takes a very specific skillset born out of an understanding of the inner workings of the industry as well as the special execution and delivery approaches that reside only in this industry sector. Let's take a look at what makes projects—and project management—so unique in the financial services industry.

CHAPTER 2:
What is a Project in Financial Services?

To understand what makes project management so unique in financial services, we should first look to answer the simple question, "What is a project?" The Project Management Institute defines a project as "a temporary endeavor undertaken to create a unique product or service." That definition is, of course, as true in financial services as it is in all industries. What makes the financial services industry unique, however, is what is involved in the *makeup* of a project.

Projects in financial services typically deliver *intangible* products through *tangible* means. What does that mean? A project in financial services—as opposed to one in construction or pharmaceuticals—often must physically construct the means through which an idea can deliver a service. For example, a financial services project manager may be tasked with something like leading the creation of a technology platform through which Family Offices[19] could centralize and optimize their services. If you compare this initiative to managing the construction of a school, the difference becomes clear. Although the tools and materials involved—such as hardware, software, training collateral, etc.—are often tangible, the actual products of most financial services projects are *intangible*. Another example of an intangible product in the financial services industry is an insurance policy. If your project is tasked with

---

[19] A family office is a private company that manages investments and trusts for a single wealthy family. Douglas, Craig M.; Todd Wollack (2007-06-08). "Case highlights family office risk". Boston Business Journal. Retrieved 2007-06-27.

defining a new type of policy, the development process may include a series of actuarial calculations, investment assumptions, and sales goals, but the actual end product will remain a concept rather than a physical artifact—an intangible object as opposed to a "something" that can be touched.

Although projects of this type occur sporadically throughout every industry, the majority of financial services projects are of this "intangible" nature. Where construction projects deliver physical structures, financial projects deliver products that can be difficult to measure in typical terms of success. While other industries deliver products that people can see, touch, and hear, financial services projects often deliver results that are measured on computer screens and 401(k) statements.

There are several common project *types* that are unique to financial services—not that they do not exist outside of that domain, but that these project categories have very specific financial services aspects.

Technology Product Development is a key project type in the financial services marketplace. Over $350 billion[20] was spent on technology projects in 2010, and $84 billion was spent on new products alone.[21] A technology product can take on many forms. It may simply be an iPhone app to allow retail brokerage clients to trade stocks and bonds away from their computers. It may be a new way to deliver an existing system or service—like financial planning tools—to your customer base through concepts such as Software as a Service (a software distribution model in which applications are hosted by a vendor or service provider and made available to customers over a network, typically the Internet[22]). Whatever the end product delivers, technology product development often involves software development.

Technology Product Improvement also is a great consumer of project resources in the financial services space. Faster, cheaper, and better are constant goals for the business, and technology is often looked at as being a key driver to achieve those goals. How much money do you think is spent on improving the functionality of such websites as Fidelity.com? Technology improvement projects are also often focused on optimizing back-office functions, where profit margins are pennies per transaction (or less) and every minor improvement in the efficiency of a process could mean the difference between profit and loss. If you are able to save a few cents per trade settlement, and you settle thousands of trades a month, it adds up.

---

[20] IT Spending in Financial Services: A Global Perspective, Celent

[21] U.S. Financial Services Industry—Securities Industry and Financial Markets Association. 2010

[22] http://searchcloudcomputing.techtarget.com/definition/Software-as-a-Service. Margaret Rouse, August 2010

Investment Product Development is a project type that is, of course, pretty well contained in the financial services space. Investment Product development doesn't necessarily mean defining new types of securities (though project management is used there as well). What it means is the development of a product or product set that facilitates the servicing of financial assets. For example, investment product development could mean the creation of a process where cash is invested overnight at a better interest rate. Or it could mean the development of a new type of Exchange Traded Fund (ETF) that captures the retune of the Standard and Poor's 500 Index, called a SPDR (the name is an acronym for the first member of the family, the **S**tandard & **P**oor's **D**epositary **R**eceipts). Whatever the product, this delivery of this type of project is often very time-sensitive (faster to market, ahead of completion), technically complex, and requires a tremendous amount of industry expertise.

Process Improvement/Redesign is a very common project type within the financial services industry, and often is an incredible consumer of both human and financial resources. The financial services industry is driven by processes. Examples of these include processes to clear checks, settle trades, print reports, reconcile statements—hundreds upon hundreds of technical and business processes. Most of these, as one would imagine, began as a manual set of activities performed by an employee or series of employees. Technology began to improve these processes, but often a company would fall into the trap of making bad processes automatic. Quickly they realized that in order to increase their capacity, and thereby increase revenue, they needed to optimize their processes. The advent of such formal approaches to process improvement such as TQM, Reengineering, and Lean increased firms' ability to look at process improvement in a structured format, and led them to focus more and more on measuring the financial impact of doing things better. Process improvement projects within the financial services industry range from small-scale, such as looking at ways to improve the flow of foot traffic at a retail bank branch during the lunchtime rush, to enterprise-wide initiatives to find the geographically perfect spot for each corporate business process worldwide and creating the global end-to-end process. Technology often aids process improvement projects, but not always.

The integration of multiple technologies and/or the conversion from one system or process to another are the major components of another typical financial services project type—*Technology Conversions/Integrations.* Logically, with the hundreds of acquisitions and mergers that have occurred (and continue to occur) within our industry over the last fifty years or so, the amount of data that has had to be converted from one system to another is mind-boggling. Take, for example, the 1998 acquisition of BankAmerica by NationsBank of Charlotte, the largest bank acquisition in history at that time. A large portion of the integration of BankAmerica was the conversion from two (or more) technology systems into one (or at least fewer) systems. Corporate systems like HR, Treasury, Payroll, and Benefits eventually had to be combined—not to mention the true business line functions like account opening, check processing, and mortgage initiation. The management of the process to combine these multiple systems and business lines has become a very common project type in financial services.

Top 20 Bank and Thrift Deals announced since January 1, 2010
Ranked by deal value at announcement

Buyer (ticker)	Target (ticker)	State	Ann. Date	Deal value ($M)	Price/tang. Book (%)
Capital One Financial Corp (COF)	ING Bank FSB	DE	06/16/11	9,000.0	102.21
BMO Financial Group (BMO)	Marshall and Ilsley Corp	WI	12/17/10	5,799.0	97.63
PNC Financial Services Group Inc. (PNC)	RBC Bank (USA)	NC	06/19/11	3,450.0	97.29
Hancock Holding Co. (HBHC)	Whitney Holding Corp	LA	12/21/10	1,768.4	163.73
Mitsubishi UFJ Financial Group Inc. (FNFG)	Pacific Capital Bancorp (PCBC)	CA	03/09/12	1,515.7	224.17
First Niagara Financial Group Inc. (FNFG)	New Alliance Bancshares Inc.	CT	08/18/10	1,498.0	165.31
Comerica, Inc. (CMA)	Sterling Bancshares Inc.	TX	01/16/11	1,028.9	229.70
Prosperity Bancshares Inc. (PB)	American State Financial Corp.	TX	01/12/12	529.2	206.39
People's United Financial Inc. (PBCT)	Danvers Bancorp Inc.	MA	01/20/11	488.9	184.10
M&T Bank Corp (MTB)	Wilmington Trust Corp.	DE	10/31/10	351.3	98.97
Susquehanna Bancshares Inc. (SUSQ)	Tower Bancorp Inc.	PA	06/20/11	342.1	149.26
Nara Bancorp Inc.	Center Financial Corp.	CA	12/09/10	286.3	NM
Susquehanna Bancshares Inc. (SUSQ)	Abington Bancorp Inc.	PA	01/26/11	273.8	124.09
Valley National Bancorp (VLY)	State Bancorp Inc.	NY	04/28/11	266.9	188.22
Cadence Bancorp LLC	Encore Bancshares Inc. (EBTX)	TX	03/05/12	251.3	240.05
Brookline Bancorp Inc. (BRKL)	Bancorp Rhode Island Inc.	RI	04/19/11	233.7	193.3
Toronto-Dominion Bank (TD)	South Financial Group Inc.	SC	05/16/10	191.6	17.07
United Bankshares Inc. (UBSI)	Centra Financial Holdings Inc.	WV	12/15/10	185.4	146.30
F.N.B Corp (FNB)	Parkvale Financial Corp.	PA	06/15/11	163.0	197.55
Eastern Bank Corp	Wainwright Bank & Trust Co.	MA	06/28/10	162.8	200.21

NM = not meaningful. The ratio is NM because this is a merger of equals.
Data as of April 23, 2012
Excludes branch deals and terminated deals
All metrics are as of announcement date.
Source: SNL Financial

Technology Selection/Implementation has also become one of the major project categories in our industry. This is primarily because of the complexity, sensitivity, and regulation involved in most of the systems and applications that support the financial services sector; changing from one to another is a major undertaking. That is why the selection and implementation of new technology has become an increasingly common project type. If your organization has been using the same investment accounting system for ten years, not only do you have ten (or more years) of data stored in that system, you probably have connected that system to countless others in your organization. Your staff is also very used to the way your old system works, what it does, and what it doesn't do. Switching to another system—even if it seems to be much easier to use, more cost efficient, and more modern in its technology—is never easy. The selection of a new system, with its requirements gathering, RFP procedures, and final evaluation process, is often a project unto itself. Once selected, implementing the new technology into the organization is again a major undertaking. Very often, staff from the vendor of the new system, whether they are managed by the company buying the system or the firm supplying it, are involved in the installation (vendor project management is a topic discussed in depth later on.)

Beyond project *type*, the **budgeting process** is one that helps define a project within financial services. Most often, very two specific project budget categories exist—***Discretionary*** and ***Maintenance.***

Discretionary projects are those identified by the organization as being important to the growth and viability of the company. From this budget, new product ideas are funded, as well as process improvement initiatives, and Research and Development ideas for future growth.

Maintenance Projects are those that are required to keep the infrastructure up and running and "keep the lights on." These include corporate system upgrades, maintenance of existing systems and processes, and often mandatory projects that are required by a regulatory body—whether internal or external.

The forces that drive the creation and execution of projects within the financial services also vary. These drivers often support new business initiatives, regulatory mandates, or the need to implement new and/or emerging technologies. Projects in financial services are usually ***Client-Driven, Market-Driven, Regulation-Driven, Competition-Driven,*** or ***New Technology–Driven.***

Client-Driven projects are initiatives done in direct response to client suggestions about products and services. The methods through which these suggestions are collected can include user groups, client satisfaction surveys, or information gathered through meetings with the organizations sales force or client service representatives. Once this information is gathered, there is usually a vetting process within the firm to review and prioritize any new product or product improvement ideas that have come from the field. These ideas may be as straightforward as a client's wish to be able to trade bonds through the company's website, or more elaborate, such as being able to deposit checks into an account from your smartphone. Each idea is evaluated using whatever criteria the company utilizes (more on that later) to choose their projects, and then execution begins.

Market-Driven projects in financial services are derived from the changing landscape of products and services that appear in the industry marketplace. Products and services, of course, have to meet customers' needs to be successful and extract premium prices from the market. Therefore, product development must be driven primarily by customers' needs rather than by technological possibilities These needs can be identified in many ways. A sales representative may have read an article about the insurance industry's trend toward bundled policies, or a formal market research study may indicate customers' desire to no longer have to go to a "brick and mortar" physical bank. Whatever the initial driver of the new product or service idea, these projects are usually evaluated using the same process utilized by other discretionary initiatives (see above), and entered into the organization's project execution pipeline.

Financial Services is a highly regulated industry. Dozens of governing bodies and laws—SEC, FDIC, Federal Reserve Sarbanes Oxley—keep customers safe and allow us to operate in a marketplace inherent with large financial risks. Still, the amount of regulation—government-mandated as well as discretionary—adds a good deal of overhead to the daily activities of a financial firm. And the regulations are always changing—whether it's a new guideline from a specific client that now wants to invest only in sustainable industries or a catastrophic event like 9/11, new regulations—and changes to older ones—are introduced daily, and must be integrated into daily industry and organizational processes. This fact drives the creation of many, many projects. Continual regulatory and compliance mandates will be top-of-mind for financial institutions this year. Financial institutions can only speculate on the effects that the CARD Act,[23] the Dodd-Frank Act,[24] the Basel III Accords,[25] and the pressure to increase transparency will have. Although the exact implications of these reforms are uncertain, institutions will have to act accordingly and plan ahead for the expenses they may entail. According to research from business advisory firm Deloitte and Touche, the top hundred financial institutions will spend over $100 billion a year on these implementations alone by 2012.[26] The financial crisis of 2008 will generate more. Often the governing bodies allow firms several years to implement and demonstrate compliance to new laws, but sometimes they do not. It becomes up to the governed organization to quickly initiate, analyze, and implement strategies around new regulations, and subsequently spawn the projects

---

[23] Credit Card Accountability Responsibility and Disclosure Act of 2009—a bill to amend the Consumer Credit Protection Act, to ban abusive credit practices, enhance consumer disclosures, protect underage consumers, and for other purposes: http://www.govtrack.us/congress/bills/111/s414

[24] The Dodd-Frank Act (fully known as the Dodd-Frank Wall Street Reform and Consumer Protection Act) is a United States federal law that places regulation of the financial industry in the hands of the government: http://searchfinancialsecurity.techtarget.com/definition/Dodd-Frank-Act

[25] Basel III is part of the continuous effort made by the Basel Committee on Banking Supervision to enhance the banking regulatory framework. It builds on the Basel I and Basel II documents, and seeks to improve the banking sector's ability to deal with financial and economic stress, improve risk management and strengthen the banks' transparency: http://www.investopedia.com/terms/b/basell-iii.asp#axzz267d109ax

[26] FinTech Marketing http://www.fintechmarketing.com/?p=669

to support them. This process is a critical driver of projects in our marketplace, and one that carries with it a large component of downside risk. If compliance to internal or external regulations is not demonstrated in a timely fashion, the very existence of the organization is in jeopardy.

Another key project category in financial services is **Competition- Driven** *projects*. These initiatives are identified and undertaken to either catch up with, better compete against, or get ahead of your direct competition is a particular product or services sector. For example, if your competition has recently begun to offer its clients the opportunity to trade stocks in Singapore, you may very quickly begin evaluating your own potential for offering the same service. Assessing a direct response to a competitor's new strategy can be tricky, however, as what may be profitable for them may not be for you. An organization may have barriers to entering certain markets, or internal rules or regulations that may not make it possible—or profitable—to develop and deliver a certain product or service.

Although catching up with your competition can be challenging, getting and staying ahead is the more daunting task, and most often involves developing strategies and initiatives through a forward-looking process that may not be natural to a financial services organization. It is very easy to look at a competitor's website and see what that competitor is doing and then decide if you should be doing that, too. It's quite another to be able to design truly *new* products and services—maybe ones that totally diverge from your current portfolio. In a highly regulated and risk-averse industry like financial services, designing and rolling out a new product or service is often dramatically different than doing so in other industries. Dozens of internal and external stakeholders are often involved even in the initial evaluation process, making it difficult to achieve any type of fast-to-market scenario. Still, new products and services are introduced every day in our industry, and they make up a good deal of the projects on which we work. Many organizations over the last several years have put in place product development methodologies that involve formal processes defining the steps a new product must go through before it is approved as a project—from initial thought to final rollout. This has helped in providing a path for new ideas that previously might have disappeared for lack of understanding of how they could become a project.

One fact that has become evident over the last several years is that *the financial services industry loves technology.* Whether it's the latest mobile device, or some high-powered program designed to predict market movements for the next ten years, people and companies in the financial services space love gadgets! According to Gartner Research, technology spending by financial firms will rise 3.6 percent in

2011 to $402 billion, as reported by Bank Technology News. That compares with 2.2 percent growth in 2010 and a 6.2 percent decline in 2009. Unfortunately, the growth rate in the financial services industry will lag the 5.1 percent growth rate of IT spending overall. Meanwhile, Ovum predicts that spending on IT vendors by financial firms will rise 4.5 percent in 2011, compared with 0.3 percent in 2010 and a 4.2 percent drop in 2009.[27] Much of this will be used in maintenance projects or in support of other new product initiatives. Projects focused on ***New Technology***, however, still take up a large part of the overall discretionary budgets of many financial institutions. New Technology projects are initiatives that focus on delivering a new platform, software, or service primarily for the sake of the actual technology. Mobile applications are a good example. The ability to check your savings account balance on your Droid device probably is not a huge money maker for such banks as Wells Fargo. Still, because the technology is new and "flashy," the company felt it had to have a presence on the new technology. The same thing can be said for "Cloud Computing" (*Internet-based computing in which large groups of remote servers are networked so as to allow sharing of data-processing tasks, centralized data storage, and online access to computer services or resources*[28]). Many financial organizations are exploring uses for this new technology, primarily to look for potential—not necessary existing—markets for the technology.

---

[27] FierceFinanceIT http://www.fiercefinanceit.com/story/it-spending-still-recovering-financial-services/2011-01-16

[28] Dictionary.com http://dictionary.reference.com/browse/cloud+computing

TIP: *Defining the project by asking the question...*

It is sometimes very difficult to get a financial services organization to admit that they have already defined and are actually working on a *project*. This phenomenon occurs for a couple of reasons—often projects emerge in operational areas that are used to "getting the widgets out the door" and not managing and delivering specific projects. Also, some companies continue to rage against the concept of project management and consider the work their staff is doing to complete these unique initiatives part of their daily responsibilities. What I've found to work exceptionally well in setting the stage for a successful project—where perhaps no project has gone before—is to ask your sponsor and key stakeholders to answer the following question:

"How will we know when we're finished?"

This simple and direct query is the most important question you can pose to your stakeholders in this situation—it will instantly help you frame into a *project* what has been to date spoken only about as "the work." Getting your sponsor and the rest of the team to think about their work as having a definitive end and delivering finite products will go a long way to helping them understand the basics elements of successful projects—and help you manage theirs.

CHAPTER 3:
What is Unique about Projects In
The Financial Services Industry

Now that we've taken a look at what defines a financial services project, let's examine what makes these projects different from projects in other industries. As I've mentioned, financial services projects often look similar to projects one may have seen outside of the industry—maybe they're integrating a system, maybe they're upgrading an enterprise software package. On the surface, these project types appear as if they could belong in any industry. In point of fact, however, financial services projects are very different.

Large Budgets are the norm—taken at face value, financial services projects can be extremely costly when compared to projects in other industries. This is due primarily to three contributing factors:

1. Financial Services projects—for the most part—have ***very large potential benefits*** associated with them... For example, you may estimate that this new trading platform is going to generate $25 million over the next three years. If that is the case, then it's really not going to matter that I'm spending $5 million this year to develop it. The same can be said for process improvement projects. If your project is going to save the bank $20,000 a month in labor costs, then the time and money you spend to get there is almost inconsequential.

2. Financial Services project are mainly ***top-line focused***—the majority of financial services projects are concerned only with the top-line benefits for which they are undertaken—usually revenue or cost savings. Much less attention is paid to the expenses associated with the project. This is ***VERY unique***, as most projects outside of our industry look at the total financial impact—measured using such tools as ROI or maybe NPV—not just the top line. The reason behind this in financial services is again because of the scale of the projects and the actual numbers on the top line of the income statement. The rationale is that the bottom line will eventually catch up with the top line. In addition, many financial services projects, particularly in large organizations, are delivered by internal project teams, and are paid for using internal charge-back or transfer pricing methods. This practice is notoriously inaccurate, and often not even used. Therefore, it is only the top line that matters.

3. ***Most Financial Services projects involve IT*** — As discussed previously, the financial services industry *loves* technology. It therefore makes sense that a good number of our projects involve IT investment, whether it's in hardware, software, or staff (internal employees or consultants).

Another unique aspect of projects in the financial services space is the fact that many of them service ***both internal and external*** clients. This can lead to competing stakeholder priorities and interests. Take, for example, developing a new stock lending application to be sold to the company's current client base. As project manager, your primary client is the internal product and sales organization that has funded your project and is waiting with bated breath for the new software. But what about your *external* client? The eventual users of the system? How are their needs being addressed? You may also have to work with the internal group responsible for rolling out/implementing the software *at* the external client. And let's take it a step further—suppose that you are a project management consultant brought in to manage the project and the internal team. Then an additional client becomes the person to whom you report and whom you must, in turn, satisfy. It gets the trickiest when the various clients are demanding completely different things and you are forced to choose an alliance. The sales and product organizations want speed to market and a commercially viable product. The external client certainly wants timely delivery, but may be more concerned with the end product's functionality and cost. You, on the other hand, must make sure that the internal sales and product organizations are satisfied, the software works as required so the external client is satisfied, and, guess what—the person who hired you also needs to be kept happy. And what keeps that person happy may be different than what is required to satisfy the others (for example, the hiring manager may need you to keep to a fixed consulting budget, but getting the work done may require substantial overtime.) This multiple-stakeholder scenario, I have found, happens more in financial services than in any other industry.

One cannot look at the uniqueness of projects and project management within the financial services industry without taking a few moments to look at the impact of corporate culture. Our industry is a strange blend of incredibly tight regulation and entrepreneurship, of cutting-edge technology and "old school" thinking, of trust and distrust. Because of these opposing forces constantly battling within our corporate cultures, the way we plan, execute, and deliver projects cannot help but be affected.

Let's start with organizational structure. As much as we'd like to think, as we move through the middle of the new millennium, that organizations are built more for execution than for bureaucracy, this is still not the case for the majority of financial services firms. Vice presidency runs rampant! The typical model of functional organizations, of supervisors, managers, assistant vice presidents, vice presidents, senior vice presidents, etc. is still the norm. People work in a functional area, are then made responsible for a team, then a department, a division, and given the task of making sure that department and that group runs efficiently. People remain in silos. If you then take this model and juxtapose it over the need to execute complex projects requiring not only multiple subject matter experts but a skillset that may not be organic to the organization (like project management!), one can see the problem. The company will most often have a very difficult time working across organizational borders, understanding the objectives of the entire enterprise, and (unfortunately for us project managers) valuing skillsets that are not their own.

Let's take that last point a step further. One key factor to remember when looking at projects and project management in financial services is that *Industry Subject Matter Expertise reigns supreme*! Your value to an organization—at least for the majority of firms—is in direct proportion to the amount of knowledge that you have acquired about specific industry functions or processes. Now, initially, that is understandable. Most financial business lines are extremely knowledge-intensive, often both technologically and from a pure nuts-and-bolts operational perspective. In order to reconcile client bank accounts, for example, you need to not only know about all the different transactions possible within these accounts and how they are processed, but also every internal system that must be reviewed and updated, every deadline and internal workflow requirement, and any banking regulations that may pertain to reconciliation. If you are looking to develop a new system for segregating the collateral received for a repurchase agreement, you're going to have to understand what all of those words mean That's not to say that a project manager cannot ever succeed without this backlog of industry expertise, but the odds do start against you. The longer a person has worked in a finite set of business or technical processes, the more valuable that person will appear to the organization. We all have had this experience—always having *the* person to call with a question on this subject or that process. Where this cultural attribute becomes counterproductive is when subject matter expertise is not supplemented with additional skillsets—again like project management!—to accomplish organizational goals not associated with day-to-day processing. We see this all of the time when a financial services firm looks to execute highly complex projects using only their existing functional staff. Though well-versed in how the company may execute a process, often these folks are *not* well-versed in how to execute a *project*, therefore leading to the Accidental Project Manager approach (*the Accidental Project Manager is a professional that accidentally, or by chance/coincidence, gets to manage a project although that was not likely a preferred career choice. Managing the project can be on a part-time or full-time basis. Once the project is complete, the professional resumes his or her normal functional duties and may never manage a project again*[29]). The majority of financial services firms feel it is easier to train a subject matter expert in project management than vice versa.

Another aspect of corporate culture unique (at least in its depth of penetration) to the financial services industry is the prevalent "hero culture." A hero culture is a corporate environment that values a person's ability to react to an emergency within the context of their business. The better their ability to react and resolve the situation, the higher in regard the person is held. Also known as a "firefighter" culture, ***this way of operating values putting out "fires" instead of preventing them.*** This, of course, has a very visible effect on projects and project management. If you think about it, a great deal of project management time is spent on either planning or anticipating. When you plan your project, you are putting in place mechanisms that will allow you to continually monitor a project's progress in regards to scope, time, and budget. Equally importantly, you are responsible for anticipating and planning for any risks that may occur—not *only* anticipating, but defining very finite management steps to execute in case these risks do occur. You do all of these processes to ***avoid*** emergencies. So the very behavior that many financial services firms reward is something we, as project managers, are trained to discourage. It's a unique situation, and one of which industry project management practitioners should be aware.

---

[29] SUKAD Project Management Knowledge Portal http://sukadipms.wordpress.com/2011/09/08/the-accidental-project-manager/

Quality management (the *fourth* of the triple constraints) also falls victim to this cultural attribute. As we all remember from our Quality classes, it is always better (and cheaper) to prevent an error than to inspect and find one. Still, the most common model in the financial services industry is wait until the process is complete, then review (inspect) and sign off. A lot of this behavior stems from the fear that someone up the line will make a mistake that only the final reviewer can catch. In this case, it can be understood, if not condoned. Our industry often places somewhat inexperienced professionals in charge of processing large financial transactions with little or no training. A sign-off (or, often, series of sign-offs) may be required by government or internal regulations or policy. Unfortunately, *project stakeholders sometimes use this process to limit their participation in a project.* They will wait until business or technical requirements are complete before "coming to the table," when their earlier participation in the *creation* of the requirements would probably have made them more complete, and most likely better overall.

Another unique element in the financial services space is the overall percentage of projects that are the direct result of government regulation. Other than the pharmaceutical industry, financial services is the industry in which the largest portion majority of all projects—IT or otherwise—are undertaken because of or due to a governing body.

Take the insurance sector, for example. Overall, it has been estimated that this financial services sector will spend over $74 billion on IT by 2015, outpacing the growth of IT spending in financial services and comprising 15 percent of total IT spending in the industry in 2012.[30] Chartis Research forecasts that the market for a single industry initiative alone—Solvency II—will grow 8 percent from $1.5 billion in 2012 to $1.67 billion in 2013 (Solvency II is European Union insurance legislation that aims to unify a single EU insurance market and enhance consumer protection.)

Compliance and risk management rules driven by governing bodies *internal* to an organization also drive the creation and execution of many industry projects. A good example of this would be a firm's internal audit department. Often this department or group will identify shortcomings in a process or procedure that will require a project to remedy. For example, the internal audit of a project that developed an online bill pay system may have identified an issue with the way the project managed the migration of software code from one technology region to another. This may cause the parent organization to choose and install a change and configuration management system in order to resolve the audit issue.

---

[30] IDC Financial Insights

2012 Risk Management IT Spending Estimates

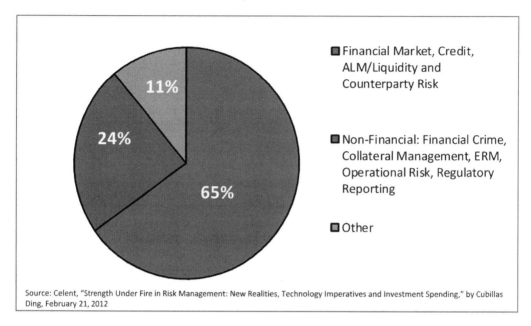

Source: Celent, "Strength Under Fire in Risk Management: New Realities, Technology Imperatives and Investment Spending," by Cubillas Ding, February 21, 2012

As I mentioned above, financial services projects very often involve new technology. This is true for a few reasons:

1. The complexity of many of the processes in financial services demands a vehicle that can capture and process large volumes of information. For example, a mutual fund company may need to price thousands of securities every day, year after year. These prices must be both accurate and timely, as regulations mandate that all fund prices must be reported after the market close at 4 p.m. In order to be able to capture, check, and publish all of this information quickly, efficient technology systems are required.

2. Many financial services processes are very repetitive and also produce very small profit margins. If these processes are to be improved, the only way to achieve any type of consistently high performing and scalable delivery mechanism is to automate and optimize the process through technology.

3. Often, financial services firms need to process or re-task legacy information, and the only way to do that efficiently is with new technology. For example, if a bank needs to offer online banking services, all of its old systems for tracking accounts must be updated to be able to be accessed by newer applications capable of moving the information to the web.

Words from the Field: "Something I Can Touch…"

An interesting observation was made by Dave R, a senior project manager at a large insurance firm in the northeast United States. Dave has spent much of his fourteen-year career in the financial services sector, but remains very active in local project management organizations that contain members from many different industries Over the years, Dave has noticed a very distinct trait in project managers who end up leaving financial services to pursue careers in other commercial areas—people who continue to practice project management and are both talented and successful. What Dave has noticed in conversations is that PMs who leave financial services long to work on projects that will produce "something I can touch." Most financial services *produce products that are intangible*, like a new type of insurance policy or mutual fund class. The industry-changers that Dave observed left to work on projects in industries like construction or manufacturing, where project deliverables can be seen and touched—often as they progress through the project's lifecycle. In order to be comfortable—long term—as a project manager in the financial services space, a person must be comfortable with projects that may deliver successful concepts…even if they remain untouchable.

CHAPTER 4:
How is "Project Success" Defined And Measured In Financial Services?

As a project management consultant, I am often asked by clients to come in and assess their project management processes. There are several methodologies or metrics I may use, but the one single question I always ask first is the simplest, yet the hardest project management question to answer—how do you define project success?

Project success within the financial services industry takes on many forms, and firms take various approaches to both defining and measuring its achievement. The majority of financial services company focus on keeping to *schedule* as a key measure of success—did we make the "date"? It is an easy metric to understand, communicate, measure, and define. Absolutely every project of which I have ever been a part was, in some way, judged by its ability to meet "the date." Unfortunately, the way that financial services firms often define and manage "the date" also varies in its process and effectiveness. More on that later.

Financial success is often spoken of when project measurement criteria are discussed. "Financial success" primarily means the project *budget*. The project budget is usually a static number that is the result of the initial planning process of the project, and is also the result of a simple mathematical process of multiplying the number (and type) of resources by their hourly (monthly, yearly) pay rate by the estimated work they are going to perform on the project. Voila—project budget. This mystical number now becomes the single financial metric against which your project is measured. The only time this number changes is when a "change control" is submitted, looking to update the budget based on a change in scope or resources. Then the new number takes the place of the old. There are, of course, several shortcomings in judging the financial success of the project on this single number, such as the often limited connection between the work actually completed and the financial performance of the project. But again—more on that later.

In a growing number of projects, a business case is developed to quantify both the creation of the project, but also how the long-term performance of the initiative will be judged. This practice is somewhat new in the financial services industry, where many a multi-million dollar project was undertaken simply because the CEO walked into a room and said, "Wouldn't it be cool if we could…"

The use of a business case, with its market analysis, quantitative and qualitative benefit definitions, cash flow projections, and project estimates was a very large step forward in the overall project delivery model for financial services projects and how we define success. There are, however, very wide interpretations of what should be included in a business case, and even more divergent thoughts on how and when the business case should be used to measure a project's performance. The business case, like many other measures initially created to assess the financial success of a project, often remains untouched after its initial creation and approval, even though dramatic changes may have occurred during the execution of the project or projects defined therein. For example, a business case may show that the defined initiative will have an internal rate of return of 5 percent based on the project being completed on time and within budget, and that the new end product can begin producing revenue within a year. Now what happens if the project is late, over budget, and not going to deliver the end product in time for any revenue generation for three years? The business case, of course, should be reviewed, updated, and approved again based on the new assumptions. This rarely occurs, and therefore affects the validity of any business case effort. Additional business case metrics like Total Cost of Ownership—a financial measurement designed to uncover all the lifetime costs of acquiring, operating, and changing an asset—are also mentioned occasionally but still not widely accepted as popular project success metrics in financial services projects. Additional detail on how Cost and Schedule are managed in financial services projects is presented in subsequent chapters.

Looking further at business-defined success criteria, the practice of Demand Management is now becoming somewhat more widespread in our industry. Demand management is the process for proactively managing project ideas and execution (demand) within the context of overall business constraints like resources, funding, etc. (supply). This process can be observed as simply as the collection of all project ideas on a standardized form up to and including enterprise software applications that walk you through the quantification of a business idea into an approved and funded project. Demand management is usually done during what most large financial services firms call the budget cycle. Each department or group makes a list of all of the projects they want to pursue this year (it is, in the vast majority of cases, an annual—process) and submit them in some form to some committee for evaluation. This "evaluation" can take on many flavors, from full-boat financial analysis to more qualitative discussions with other senior department staff. More often than not, however, the firm lacks a set of *objective criteria* against which all projects project could be evaluated. Measures like ROI, IRR, NPV, Payback period, market perception, strategic fit, etc. that could be used to look objectively at a project proposal are seldom utilized It often comes down to a few senior managers sitting in a meeting and making deals that if we do "your" project first, then we can do my project…we'll split the resources, and I will give you 75 percent of the overall budget for the year if I can have Sally from your team to manage my project. It is often the case, unfortunately, that this legacy process stands in the way of any true strategic progress, as the company's goals and objectives are not used in evaluating whether or not a project should be allowed to consume valuable resources—human, financial, as well as technical and physical—that may be better suited for another initiative.

Project execution—or really more project *status*—is often used as a measure of success in the world of financial services project management. These point-in-time measurements that may be available to a project manager are often used to assess the overall health of a project, and if the project will truly deliver on its expected benefits. Let's take a look at how this measurement process may also include a few shortcomings.

One project execution measurement is what we've all come to know as "actuals" "What are our actuals versus our estimates?" This term could refer to several project attributes, such as budget, milestones, or interim project deliverables. Project execution metrics also offer a very easily understood language as to project success, and stakeholders usually flock to these project measurements. It is easy to comment on a project being over/under budget, behind/ahead of schedule/ and late with producing final documentation. Yes—all are easy to understand, but often misinterpreted as to their importance unless evaluated together and in the proper context.

Take your project budget for example. If you are able to capture actuals (the cost of your resources and their effort for a given time period or deliverable) you will also be able to compare the money spent (these actuals) against the money you should have spent to date. The questions that revolve around these comparisons are numerous. In one example, you may be under budget to date, but you also have not completed any of the deliverables that were due for this time period. Therefore, although financially you may seem to be on-track, your project is actually behind schedule... if your stakeholders are just focused on the budget numbers, their perception of the project may be a little skewed.

The same misconception of project status can also be drawn in the case of allowing singular focus on unrealistic milestones. In this case, the issue is reversed. Your stakeholders may be in ecstasy, seeing that your development phase has been completed on time. But they may miss the fact that it cost three times the budgeted amount and delivered half of the expected functionality. This again is an issue of only seeing half of the picture.

If project success is being judged only by the timeliness of the completion of interim deliverables, this once more could paint an inaccurate picture. Here, though, it's possible to see a status that is less positive than is truly the case. Often traditional waterfall methodologies insist that each set of phase-end deliverables be complete and approved or signed off before the next project phase can begin. This approach can produce what appear to be delays but are actually normal (and sometimes productive) progress. In the simplest case, the time it can sometimes take to have numerous stakeholders—often in multiple physical locations—approve and sign off on project documentation can take time. Unfortunately, this time can appear on your project status reports as a delay in completing your deliverables. If your stakeholders are just looking at dates and not digging down further, this will at least drive additional questions and conversations.

Assessing a project's success only in terms of interim project deliverables can also have stakeholders scratching their heads—especially when project methodologies employ delivery approaches that may be unfamiliar. This can be the case when your team is using an Agile method for the first time.

An Agile approach to projects is based on four major tenets—individuals and interactions over processes and tools, working software over comprehensive documentation, customer collaboration over contract negotiation, responding to change over following a plan[31]. Whether your project is following a full Agile approach, or

---

[31] Manifesto for Agile Software Development, 2001, Kent Beck, Mike Beedle, Arie van Bennekum, Alistair Cockburn, Ward Cunningham, Martin Fowler, James Grenning, Jim Highsmith, Andrew Hunt, Ron Jeffries, Jon Kern, Brian Marick, Robert C. Martin, Steve Mellor, Ken Schwaber, Jeff Sutherland, Dave Thomas

just looking to utilize a method that calls upon an Agile way of thinking, often the tactics used in completing interim project deliverables are unique. It is often the case that requirements documents, for example, are not complete until development is done. Agile or Extreme project methodologies also often have development and testing being done simultaneously with the full-time participation of the business owner, so completing full-blown test plans in anticipation of a testing cycle may not make sense. This, again, can be difficult for a firm—used to very sequential project phases and a well-defined path of interim deliverables—to grasp. If you are used to judging a project's success by the progress and completion of such interim deliverables, then a non-traditional project lifecycle will be a challenge.

Reasons for Adopting Agile Methods[32]

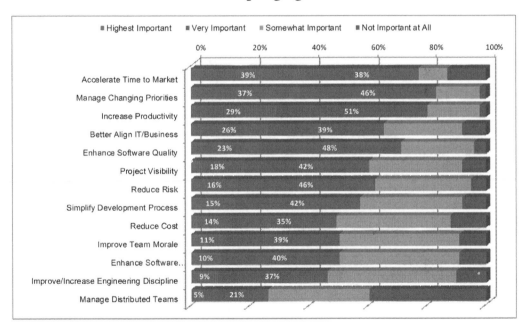

As mentioned above, a singular focus on any standard project metric can yield inaccurate assessments of a project's interim and ultimate success. Unfortunately, a method that *does* combine several of the aforementioned measurements—budget, schedule, and actuals—is rarely used in financial services project management. This measurement is ***earned value***—the fairly simple concept that clearly links work that was expected to be done and the time it was expected to take with the actual progress

---

[32] State of Agile Development Survey Results. VersionOne, http://www.versionone.com/ state_of_agile_development_survey/11/

made in terms of what has been completed and the effort spent. The application of this concept, however, is not often seen—perhaps because it may appear to be too quantitative for most projects to address. *Often project management in financial services means applying the "easiest to understand" methods and techniques.* This is because many project sponsors view project management as a necessary evil, but want to keep these evil processes in check. Earned value—and other quantitative project management methods and tools—can be seen as unnecessary work and looked upon as simply additional overhead.

An additional measure of project success often used in financial services is the simple "Star Trek" method—i.e. "check-off" (after Pavel Chekov of the Starship Enterprise)[33]. This approach uses the company's (or the project manager's) map of milestones and deliverables as a one hundred percent must-execute mandatory road-map for a successful project. Each activity, each stage gate, each milestone and phase is looked upon as being equally important to the completion of the project, and therefore an absolute must for a successful project. The project manager then proceeds to "check off" each and every phase as it is completed—whether the work adds value to the project or not. This is often the method used when organizations are somewhat new to project management or formal methodologies and have not had the chance to evaluate the flexibility that might be available. Projects will view every step, every deliverable, as compulsory, and therefore be judged simply by their completion—even if the activities are not necessary, or worse, detrimental to the successful completion of the project.

The measure of project success that is used in almost every financial services project is stakeholder satisfaction—are the sponsor and appropriate stakeholder constituencies happy? This method also helps define what additional measures of success should be used by understanding and capturing what is success to them. Maybe your sponsor only cares about the delivery date. Maybe the end users are totally focused on the functionality of the product and could wait a few weeks if the product was right. The budget may be the one component that the PMO cares about. Whatever the project, whatever the situation—stakeholder happiness is a critical measure of financial services project success.

The most important thing to remember in understanding how project success is measured in the world of financial services is that, depending on the situation, every

---

[33] Pavel Andreievich Chekov (Russian: Павел Андреевич Чехов) is a Russian Starfleet officer in the Star Trek fictional universe. Walter Koenig portrayed Chekov in the original Star Trek series and first seven Star Trek films; Anton Yelchin portrayed the character in the 2009 film Star Trek..; http://en.wikipedia.org/wiki/Pavel_Chekov

approach is valid. *There is no incorrect way to measure project success if the performing organization and appropriate stakeholders are in agreement.* We may think that one method or another is short-sighted, or outdated, or mathematically incorrect. What's important here is that financial services firms judge project success differently, and we, as project managers must be able to deliver projects that succeed *in the terms of our stakeholders.*

Depending on the project, business line, stakeholder and expectations, certain success criteria may be used. For example, financial services software vendors will primarily use timeline and quality. That is because the faster the software is delivered (in quality form) to the end user, the sooner the firm can begin to recognize revenue from maintenance fees. Investment management firms almost exclusively use timeline, and for similar reasons. The faster they can get a new project completed, the faster they too can begin generating revenue from the results of the initiative. In these examples, managing project costs can be secondary, as usually the anticipated revenue from an investment management-approved project is substantial. A project done to fulfill a regulatory requirement—another common project type for investment managers—also would focus on timeline, as getting these implemented by a certain date is the law.

The criteria used to evaluate the success of projects in the *consulting* sector usually revolve around budget and timeline. Budget is important here for a couple of reasons. From the consultant's side, most projects are done against an agreed-upon budget negotiated with the client. Should the consultant start to approach exhausting that budget, and not be near finished with the contracted work, difficult conversations are sure to follow. The same can be said with regard to the timeline—if the consultant has committed to certain timeframes, and they are not going to be met, then the consultant will need to address the situation with the client. The client has the same concerns as the consultant, but with a slightly different "take." The budget that the client has negotiated with the consultant has now become part of the overall expectation-set of the project, and of his/her performing organization. That means that if the consultant hired to do the work is going to go over budget, the hiring manager will have to explain it to his/her own stakeholders. The same can be said with any timeline delays. Both the consultant and the client want to be successful in terms of budget and timeline, but for different reasons.

When one examines success criteria for projects being done at the larger financial institutions such as large custody banks, insurance companies, or mutual fund conglomerates, one traditionally sees adherence to schedule as the cornerstone of these evaluations. This is because much of the work done on these projects was formerly done by internal resources, and tracked financially by an internal sort of transfer pricing method than often meant little more to people than random numbers on a spreadsheet. This has changed dramatically since the financial crisis of 2008. Many of these same firms are now trying to institute strict cost control measures to manage project budgets as well as timelines. Unfortunately, what is often happening is that the *systems and processes the companies have in place are insufficient to collect and decipher the data* that the firm's executives now say they need. It will take several years before these internal processes catch up and give these institutions a truly integrated financial management process for their projects.

TIP: *Different Success Criteria for Different Stakeholder Groups*

The current head of the PMO for a business group at one of the top three U.S. insurance companies often recommends to his project managers the practice of defining and managing *two distinct sets of project success criteria*—**Strategic and Tactical**—for the delivery of mission critical projects. Tactical success criteria focus on what we all traditionally know as the "triple constraints"—time, cost, and scope—and are usually the measures of success used for the direct project team and the immediate recipient of the final deliverables of the initiative. In measuring tactical success criteria, timely completion of milestones, adherence to budget, and traceability of requirements to functionality all are used to continually assess the state of the project throughout its lifecycle. This process is probably familiar to all of us, and would be expected in most projects.

What was interesting was the discussion he and I had about a totally separate set of *Management Success Criteria.* In using this evaluation approach, senior management of the performing organization creates—either formally or informally—measurement criteria against which **they** will judge the success or failure of the project. These metrics may be qualitative (example—how is the organization *reacting* to the implementation of a new payroll system), quantitative (budget, timelines, etc.), or both. There are, however, two very distinct and significant attributes of these management success criteria

1. *The measures may be dramatically different than the metrics being used by the project team*—management may have different expectations of their organization, and therefore may judge the success of a project differently. A simple example would be: the project team may have a schedule that shows the final deliverable date of August 15th. Management may feel that they would be satisfied with a date of October 15th.

2. *The metrics are unknown to the project team*—for the most part, Management Success Criteria are discussed and reviewed only by those who create them. This practice, of course, has its good and bad points. On the positive side, senior management may be more forgiving of a mistake or delay by the project team, as management's expectations may be more lenient than those of the team. Negatively, though, the existence of these two metric sets can affect the overall performance

of the project team and the project itself. If the team feels that management is set on a specific date or timeline, for example, they may execute their activities in a different (and less than effective) manner than if they knew that their bosses really had given them more time.

The key lesson here is that stakeholder management may be more flexible in their assessment of project success than the project team themselves. Senior leaders often are as interested in how the team develops organizationally as they are in very stringent (and more traditional) measurements of scope, time and cost. Dependent on such attributes as organizational culture, project size, and project type, success may be judged very differently.

CHAPTER 5:
Project Delivery in the Financial Services Industry

While the criteria for assessing project success vary greatly in the financial services industry, it is in the way projects are *delivered* that our firms illustrate the most diversity. Numerous organizational models, methodologies, and knowledge requirements are used to execute the many types of projects of which we've spoken. Again, situational requirements, as well as the company's industry sector and ingrained culture, impact these methods.

Organizational models drive project execution in the financial services industry more than any other component. Project delivery models vary greatly here, from centralized Project Management Organizations (PMO) to traditional decentralized business-line owned project managers. In year 2000 research done by ESI, only 47 percent of companies had a project office. In 2006, research showed that 77 percent of companies had a PMO; in 2010, 84 percent; and in 2012, 87 percent of companies had PMOs. The defined duties and responsibilities of a PMO, however, span the range from just providing centralized project reporting to being the firm's center for organizational strategy. Current research shows that PMO activities include providing common methodology and vocabulary, guiding and mentoring project managers, sharing knowledge, defining roles and responsibilities, assessing and auditing projects, supporting team development, assisting in project recovery, monitoring business performance and management, and assisting in the career pathing of project managers, as well as providing measurements and metrics, tools, process expertise, training, and development.

So what is a simple description of a PMO? A Project Management Office (PMO) is a group or department within a business, agency or enterprise that defines and maintains standards for project management within the organization.[34] How a PMO is designed and staffed for maximum effectiveness depends on a variety of organizational factors, including targeted goals, traditional strengths, and cultural imperatives. There are three basic organizational styles for a project management office:[35]

1. *The project repository*—occurs most often in organizations that empower distributed, business-centric project ownership, or enterprises with weak central governance. The project office simply serves as a source of information on project methodology and standards. Project managers continue to report to, and are funded by, their respective business areas.

2. *The project coach model*— assumes a willingness to share some project management practices across business functions and uses the project office to coordinate the communication. Best practices are documented and shared and project performance is monitored actively. The PMO in this model is a permanent structure with staff and has some supervisory responsibility for all projects.

3. *The enterprise project management office*—also assumes a governance process that involves the project office in all projects, regardless of size, allowing it to assess scope, allocate resources and verify time, budget, risk, and impact assumptions before the project is undertaken. Funding is generally a combination of direct, budgeted allocation for baseline services and a fee-for-service charge for others.

Whatever the model, the presence and function of a PMO within a financial services organization has a large impact on the way projects are executed and delivered.

Many financial services firms still use a de-centralized model, where projects are managed by staff members of the department most affected by the project. Sometimes, this person is a full-time project manager, but more often than not, this poor soul is what has been termed "the accidental project manager"—really a project manager by chance, not by choice. This often less-than-effective process for assigning project leadership is driven by the fact that *the financial services industry values subject matter expertise over project management knowledge*. Most firms would rather have an

---

[34] http://searchcio.techtarget.com/definition/Project-Management-Office

[35] http://searchcio.techtarget.com/definition/Project-Management-Office

extremely experienced staff member "hack" their way through project management activities than vice versa. This is changing a little, as project management is becoming a core professional competency (like financial management or marketing) and may soon be expected to be part of a person's standard skillset. Still, there are pockets of accidental project managers running around. Decentralized project delivery models also exist with trained project managers, too. Often, this type of organization will have something of a decentralized PMO, where a business unit or function will have a stable of project managers to lead initiatives within that section of the company. These project managers are often recruited from within that department, but because they may have to venture beyond their core subject knowledge area—and they are most likely assigned to manage projects close to full-time—they are usually given either project management training or a suite of tools, methods, and processes to help them manage projects.

Another common model of project delivery is a stand-alone department focused on a single or several stages in a project lifecycle. This group may include project managers, business and systems analysts, and testing specialists. Technology staff are usually not housed in this group. This type of department acts as a shared service within a large organization to deliver to other parts of the firm the specific staff and skills necessary to support the project in question. Most often, a project team is constructed from departmental personnel, including a project manager, possibly an analyst or two, and maybe QA staff if required. But occasionally, individual staff members are assigned to these initiatives. This centralized group—maybe a little short of a full PMO (again, this depends on the definition of PMO)—will receive requests from various parts of the larger organization to assign resources. The process here for assigning the right resources to the right project at the right times can often be somewhat ill-defined, and may also be combined with a less than perfect project prioritization process and resource allocation/tracking system. It is the responsibility of the management of such a group to understand the priorities of the organization, and be able to manifest those in a project delivery model and in the way resources are committed. Not always the easiest thing to do.

It's also been a long-standing tradition that project management in large financial institutions resided in the information technology departments. It was always thought that IT staff were more used to working in a project-based environment, and that, since most financial projects involve IT, it made sense for them to manage the project. This has changed over the last five to seven years. During this time, there has been a trend for financial organizations to begin to define a role titled *Business Project Manager*. It is the job of the Business Project Manager to shepherd the project from the creation of the business case through project execution all the way into the marketing, sales, and client training areas. This was, and is, something of a challenging role, as most systems and processes for managing projects—like time tracking, SDLC's—have been developed to work with the IT organization. Still, having a project manager looking out for the business side of a project certainly does have its strong points. After all, aren't most projects done for business reasons?

Project delivery methodologies also exhibit great variety in the financial services world—there is more than just the run-of- the- mill "waterfall" SDLC. For projects that involve software development, though, "waterfall" is the most common approach. Most large organizations have developed over the years—whether internally or through the use of external consultants—a fairly solid set of activities and deliverables that take them through standard steps of planning, requirements, development, testing, and implementation. Not much differs from firm to firm—at least the ones using "waterfall" as the mainstay of their methodologies. Even the major deliverables look the same—same font, structure, and so on. What differs greatly from organization to organization is the advocacy, support, and governance around the use of the methodology. This is, of course, a function of both the project delivery structure (see above) and the business line and industry sector of the performing organization. A waterfall approach fits very nicely with some of the "old school" firms that appreciate the perceived order and manageability of very well-defined steps, documentation, and approval. This type of project methodology is also very easy to present to both internal and external auditors—the ever-present governing body of financial firms. Because of this, most project auditing methodologies are based on a waterfall approach. In addition, the order and standardization of this project approach lends itself to straightforward budgeting processes (example: requirements will cost X and start in April, development will cost Y and begin in July), and has therefore become the foundation for many companies' time tracking and project management tools (more on this later). For all these reasons, as well as the long-standing and well-established history of the waterfall approach, it is by far the most accepted and prevalent delivery methodology in financial services. But it is not the only one.

Agile development (we mentioned it briefly in our discussion of project success factors) came together from looking at what it would be like to deliver software faster using self-directed work teams, less documentation, and real-time collaboration between business owners, analysts, developers, and testers. Agile promised faster time-to-market, and significantly reduced times between when a software requirement was talked about and when it actually became working software. Agile development became extremely popular, to the point where technology research giant Gartner predicted that 80 percent of software development projects will use agile development methods by the end of 2012.[36]

Agile as a project delivery methodology does, however, face an uphill climb for wide-spread acceptance in financial services. This is true in any highly regulated field as well. The amount of scrutiny projects receive—both during and after execution—makes it extremely difficult to effectively use an agile approach. The capture and use of business requirements is a good example. Traditional "waterfall" approaches spend a great deal of time trying to capture every possible business requirement for a project up front, then take another period of time making sure that these are documented properly, signed off and approved by a multitude of stakeholders, communicated to the next team down the line, and properly archived in the project repository. Any changes to those requirements will go through a "change control" process, which most likely includes additional documentation, sign-offs, communication, and archiving. It all seems so orderly. More importantly, it all seems so *auditable*. As mentioned above, *much of what is done in a financial institution is done with the thought that someone will come back and question it.* The audit mentality is especially prevalent in project execution, where traceability to any decision must be present in case the decision causes harm to the organization or its clients. It is often a climate of professional fear—a climate of risk aversion, decision aversion, and consensus overload.

Now compare that environment to one of an Agile organization. In Agile, project teams are empowered to make and implement decisions within the group without seeking consensus from management or steering committees. Documentation is minimal, requirements are often one or two sentences, and change is not controlled, but embraced. Time is not tracked to a monthly budget—every few weeks or so the team is expected to produce shippable software. Period. Project plans are not constantly updated, and neither is earned value. As an Agile team, you have a "burndown" list of requirements. You choose the ones that can be developed in the time until the next release, and you develop them.

One can see immediately the cultural shock an agile approach might bring to an organization. The issue really comes down to the simple matter of trust. One of the twelve basic principles of agile development is "Build projects around motivated individuals. Give them the environment and support they need, and trust them to get the job done."[37] Yet one of the basic principles around financial services organizations is

---

[36] Pmi.org Must-Have Skill: Agile, 28 February 2012, http://www.pmi.org/en/Professional-Development/Career-Central/Must_Have_Skill_Agile.aspx

[37] The Twelve Principles Behind the Agile Manifesto

that every major decision must be reviewed and verified. This mismatch is the basis for why true agile development methods will not be widely accepted. The approach will (and has) found pockets of success—mostly around smaller development initiatives. For now, however, waterfall is king.

Agile versus Waterfall Mindset[38]

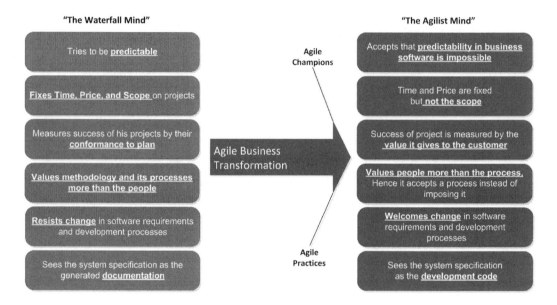

Another project methodology taking hold in the financial services marketplace is LEAN. Lean Project Management is a project strategy for achieving significant, continuous improvement in the performance of the total business project *by eliminating wastes of time and other resources that do not add value to the final project* delivered to the corporate structure.[39] What lean project management does is look to speed up the delivery of projects by eliminating any non-essential steps and moving as many decision points as possible as late in the project as possible. Lean also focuses on measurement and metrics, especially financial value. Another guiding principle of Lean Project Management is *maximizing the value differential between the corporate resources disbursed during the project versus the value received by the company* both during and

---

[38] http://mike2.openmethodology.org/wiki/Agile_Business_Transformation

[39] Ronald Mascitelli, Building a Project-Driven Enterprise: How to Slash Waste and Boost Profits Through Lean Project Management

after the life of the project.[40] Capturing data during the execution phase of the project becomes very important.

Many financial services firms, particularly in this time of reduced budgets and headcounts, tend to look toward a lean approach to deliver their projects. Fundamentally, Lean is about eliminating waste. Some waste is unavoidable, but the objective is to identify all activities that are non-value-added, and reduce as many as possible. General examples of waste include over-producing, waiting, defects and rework, over-processing, inventory, motion, and transport. A few specific examples of waste sometimes found in financial services include:

- Rework due to lost files or processing errors
- Over-processing due to duplicate client records, or redundant data entry requirements
- Movement due to physical dispersion of process participants
- Printing, copying, and transporting documents instead of transmitting and storing them electronically

Identifying, eliminating, or reducing such waste will enable firms to improve productivity, redeploy resources, increase customer satisfaction, and reduce costs.[41]

Much of the focus—and the funding—of project methodologies in financial services has been on the activities that directly produce the project deliverables. Areas such as requirements gathering and software development have always been places where concise and finite instructions could be developed on how to efficiently complete and measure each task. Recently, however, there has been a trend in financial services toward the implementation of *product* management methodologies.

Product management methodologies differ from those of the project management variety by focusing on clearly defining the products that should be developed, making sure that the products are being constructed in line with client and market requirements, and shepherding the product and its support system through development to the customer. The product development methodology is concerned only with the business value that a product will deliver, not necessarily with how it will be produced. This framework begins with defining a process through which ideas are vetted and approved, business cases are written, project parameters are defined, marketing and sales strategies are set, and final products are brought to market. A product management methodology works hand-in-hand with the project management

---

[40] Ibid.
[41] Banking Industry Leverages LEAN Principles To Eliminate Waste, A North Highland White Paper by Chad Carmichael, Scott Mullen, and Ernst-Jan Mante

methodology—one is focused on defining the vehicle through which business value will be delivered, the other with building it.

There are, of course, other delivery methodologies at work in financial services—most some type of hybrid of the ones mentioned above. The most important thing to remember here, though, is that the overarching theme in delivery of most significant initiatives is risk avoidance. Financial services is operated on the premise that everything one does is reviewable—it has to be. With the recent crisis and regulations thrust upon us over the last few years, the way we look back at projects is as equally important as the way we proceed forward with them.

STORIES FROM THE FIELD: *Financial Software Delivery as a Medical Service?*

A very good friend who runs the professional services group for a large financial systems vendor (and has twenty-plus years of industry experience) makes a unique comparison between the delivery of enterprise financial applications and the preparation and performance of a medical procedure. He contends that, in many organizations, the software vendor firm fails to acknowledge that the services team is truly an extension of the product team. He equates this to *"paying the nurse for your surgery."*

In his analogy, the "patient" (in this case the client) consistently interacts with the "nurse" (services team) to effectively implement software within patient organization. Interactions between these two groups include everything from project planning to designing new functionality for the software. For these services, the patient is presented with a (usually) large bill for services rendered.

But isn't there another process participant that may be as much or even more responsible for the success of a patient's overall outcome (or the success of a software implementation project)? Isn't it really the "doctor"? Isn't it really—in this case—the Product Development team?

Yet, my friend has observed, there is seldom any interaction between the vendor's professional services and their own product development teams. Even worse, the services team often acts as an insulating organization, never connecting the client (patient) with the person(s) who have the most direct impact on their satisfaction—the software developer (doctor). It is this disconnect that often leads to lengthening timelines, cost overruns, and eventual software solutions that do not fully meet client expectations.

CHAPTER 6:
The Role of Project Management In The Financial Services Industry

Project Management, as a function in the financial services industry, has many different flavors and many different definitions. In some firms, project management is seen as a competitive advantage in being able to deliver new products or services in a way that is managed and predictable. In other firms, however, project management is viewed almost as a necessary evil. The function or role is mandated either at a higher corporate level or by auditors to whom the firm needs to demonstrate the existence of project management. Most of the time, the role of project management in a financial services firm becomes the product of the requirements defined by the organization, the abilities and talents of the individuals performing the role, and the cumulative results and reactions of the projects done to date.

One function of project management that is prevalent in the financial services industry is *project definition.* It is almost always up to the project manager to lead the organization in creating a framework around the project's key deliverables and timeframes. Often the project manager is called upon to define the very concept of project management for the organization. This is the case where a business or operations area is looking to execute a particular initiative and has little to no experience in any type of project work. The project manager here is called upon to assist the firm in understanding what a project is, how one works on and delivers a project, and, most importantly, how it differs from the day-to-day operations of their standard work. Once this is made clear, the project manager can then proceed to finalizing the approach, methodology, and metrics that will be required to successfully deliver the project. The definition of the overall boundaries, methods, metrics, and deliverables of every project are a critical function of project managers in our industry.

Another key function of financial services project management is ***project coordination and administration.*** Although many of us do not like to admit it, I'm sure we've all worked for companies that see project management as an administrative function. All a project manager does, they say, is set up meetings, update issues lists, create Gantt charts, and draw PowerPoint slides. And in a lot of these firms, that is what a project manager does. Project management has evolved into these often necessary but inconsequential tasks because, more often than not, project management is being used at all only because it is a requirement of the organization—a mandate from an audit function or organizational PMO, or perhaps just a senior manager who has heard project management is the next "big thing." For whatever reason, project management is being viewed as a way to administer a project, not lead it. Unfortunately, this approach becomes a self-fulfilling prophecy—project management is now judged as being a purely administrative function because it's only being used as one.

Project leadership is also a common (and important) role exhibited by project management in financial services, and one that probably best serves both the delivering organization as well as the stakeholders and sponsor. In this evolution of project management, the project manager is viewed as the person responsible for delivering what was promised to the sponsor of the project. The project manager is the central contact point, responsible for not just completing deliverables and lists, but for creating and maintaining an organizational delivery mechanism that takes an idea and turns it into a physical reality. Project management as a leadership function uses what is probably the most important skillset in a project manager—communication—and leverages that ability to motivate and manage team members and diverse stakeholders into agreeing upon project deliverables and timeframes, budgets, and resources. It's been said that management is doing things right, while leadership is doing the right things. Often, project managers are called upon to do both. Luckily, when our profession is viewed as a true leadership function, we can.

The role of project management as an ***organizational requirement*** can, at its worst, cost the delivering organization a great deal of time and money and, at its best, force a company to at least give "lip service" to the concept of project management. For numerous reasons, some firms demand that projects of certain size or that impact certain business lines have a project manager assigned, and/or follow a certain methodology and produce pre-defined deliverables. The reasons, as mentioned above, may be because of audit requirements, the parent firm's standard practices, or a senior stakeholder on your project prefers the use of project management over whatever the current delivery process is. For whatever reason, *project management as an organizational mandate more often than not impedes the progress of a project.* The mandatory completion of certain project steps and deliverables—whether or not they are appropriate to the specific project type—is a standard symptom of this. Examples of this might be the rule that all projects must complete the fifteen-page Project Charter template, even though your project involves the simple addition of three web pages, or the mandate that every project produce detailed business requirements documentation, even for initiatives that simply are installing out-of-the-box software. Part of the issue with mandated project management—even if it is the right thing to do—is that the team feels that much of the control of how the project will be executed has been removed from their hands. If they are experienced in project management, they may feel that they should really be the ones defining the methods through which the project is delivered. They may question every step, thinking they have a better way. If the team is inexperienced, they may feel that the "art of project management" is really about filing out weekly status reports, tracking issues, and making sure that appropriate stakeholders are invited to every meeting (even if they have no intention of coming). If project management (or its components) is a requirement, often it is not governed beyond the simplest form. This might involve a simple inquiry like "are you using the requirements template?" or "have you finished the SDS (Systems Development Specifications) phase yet?" There most likely will not be any review of the quality of the process, as long as one can say that the deliverables, or phases, or tasks are completed. This type of "check off" (or Star Trek) project management may result in a project that is easier to track in terms of standard organizational metrics, but may also result in extra effort and cost in competing unnecessary work, and may delay completion of a project for no other reason than corporate policy.

The role of project management in financial services has certainly matured over the last several years. Where we are still hoping to make greater strides, however, is in the position of **business leadership**. Project management is still most often seen as just a tactical response to a business idea that has been defined and is in need of execution. Seldom is the project manager truly involved in the business strategy process. I don't mean as a business subject matter expert, as the ongoing debate over which is more important—subject matter or project manager expertise—is not being discussed here. What we're talking about here is being involved in the decision-making process for the organization as a whole—having the input of how project management and execution would add value to the organization beyond guiding projects through their phases. Whether it's Demand Management, Project Portfolio Management, or simply offering variations on how projects might be costed or accounted for, project management struggles for a seat at the corporate table, except possibly where project management is the major product that the firm delivers (like a software implementation or industry consulting firm). Where we are now showing improvement is the in the area of a PMO's contribution to business strategy. PM Solutions' 2012 report "State of the PMO 2012" says that 62 percent of their respondents have their PMOs participate in their overall business strategy process. Business leadership is still fighting to be part of the role of project management in financial services firms, but it may become more important as the skill becomes more of an expected core competency for all senior executives. The understanding of the importance of project management in all business decisions will continue to grow.

High Performers Deliver More Business Value than Low Performers

High performing organizations are defined by the extent they realize their organizational goals. Organizations rated themselves on a scale from 1to 5, where 1=to no extent, 5=to a very great extent. High performers rank in the top 25% in overall performance; low performers rank in the bottom 25%.

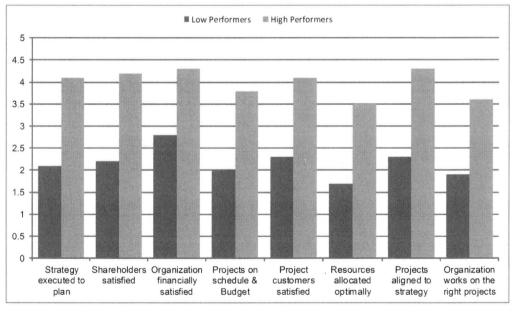

2010 Project Management Solutions

Another area where project management in financial services might not be positioned as well is in the areas of ***empowerment and accountability***. Project managers are usually responsible for ensuring that a project is set up well, that all project management processes (communications, issues, risk management, and so on) are in place, and that dates and budgets are being met. But beyond that, the project manager is seldom actually accountable for the success of the project and its ultimate deliverable. Sure, project managers are often blamed for unsuccessful projects, but how much control did they really have? For the most part in financial services, project teams do not organizationally report to the project manager in any real terms. There may be talk of matrix management, even to the point of having project managers have input into team members' reviews. But it's just that—input into a review that someone else delivers. The project manager has little or no true say in the direction the team members take beyond the time allotted by them to work on their project. Often, resources will be assigned work not related to the project for emergency reasons by their line managers. The project manager has little say, and is usually without recourse but to warn that "the project will now be delayed." Not only does the project manager have little control over the resources assigned to the project, the manager often has even less control over the actual people who will be working on the team. Most financial services firms use the shared services model, where many functions—like IT, QA, or Business Analysis—are centralized. Groups and departments then come to the centralized groups to staff their projects. But resources are more often assigned based on pure availability than on necessary skillset or "fit." This can result in less than optimally performing teams, and frustrated project managers.

But lack of true empowerment goes beyond resource management. For the many reasons mentioned above, it is very rare that project managers in financial services have any say as to the method through which they deliver projects. Methodologies—for the most part—are pre-defined for the project manager. Even if the project manager has an idea for a better way to execute a particular project, this idea may be squelched in favor of following the corporate methodology.

With this somewhat bridled level of empowerment also comes a low level of true accountability. How often is a project manager in a large (or small) financial services firm ever fired for a failed project? If the project has enough visibility, the project manager may take some "heat" but probably will not be fired. There is no true accountability for the project. In some circles, this might be seen as a plus. If all the above is true, then the project manager really shouldn't be held accountable. After all, the manager has no control of the resources that will be assigned to the project team or whether they will always be available. The manager also has little control of how the project can be delivered. With all of this out of the project manager's control, how can the manager be accountable? This is the stance of many a project manager and project management group in financial services. If this is to change, financial firms must view project managers as capable business people, with the talent and ability to make project decisions within the context of the company's vision and policy. If this becomes the case, then project managers will proudly take full accountability for the overall success of their projects.

In project execution, the role of project management in financial services firms usually takes attributes from all of the functions mentioned above, and forms a hybrid approach based on the unique needs of the firm's business lines and the projects they perform. Every organization assumes that project management, as a basic function, will be responsible for project setup. Project management will create the framework, prepare the deliverables strategy and timeline, and complete the initial budget. Also, once underway, project management will assume the role of project administration. There will also—even in the most project management–savvy organizations—be a level of mandated project management activity handed down from some governing body that must be followed, whether the project manager agrees with it or not. Resources will be assigned whether the project manager likes it or not…then they will be re-assigned off the project, and replaced with additional resources about which the manager knows little to nothing. There will be some opportunity to lead the project as the project manager sees fit, but true empowerment will most likely be superseded by the internal project processes already in place and expected by senior management.

One very important role of project management in a financial services firm is to ***advocate and publicize project management as a discipline and a best practice***. This may not always be easy—especially in firms where project management is just something somebody does in their spare time. Communicating the importance of project management and the best practices within the discipline are key functions for all financial services project managers as our profession grows.

The last financial services project management function that we will discuss is that of ***business development***. This is found primarily within the consulting world—whether it's strategy, software, or staff augmentation consulting. It is often up to the project manager to "mine" for new business within the current client base, and also develop and deliver pre-sales presentations on the firm's capabilities and approach.

The many roles of project management within the financial services space are truly an expression of the culture and organizational history of the business lines within our industry domain. Some organizations welcome the use of project management as a strategic tool to further their business initiatives, while others see project management as just a bureaucracy that must be served in order to perform within their own company. More and more, however, true project management is becoming an accepted tool within our industry, where firms are beginning to realize that the discipline is substantially more than Gantt charts and issues lists.

TIP: Project Management is in the Eye of the Beholder

MS Project does not equal project management (although many think that it does). As a project management consultant, this author has observed that, to some financial firms, having a copy of MS Project 2007 installed on their desktops equals PMI certification. What is unusual is that this concept is often partnered with the ongoing complaint "we have MS Project, but no one uses it." A paradox? Unfortunately, many companies buy and distribute MS Project licenses in support of a somewhat misguided thought process:

1. We have MS Project.

2. MS project is used by project managers.

3. Therefore, we have project managers.

4. And therefore, we must have project management.

What often follows is an organizational condition where the software application acts as *a security blanket of project management commitment.* Here true PM techniques and principles are often never learned (nor their application). Firms use the "accidental project management" approach and throw a few activities into an .mpp file.

As a consultant, I have found that the most important thing to remember is this—***project management is in the eye of the beholder*** (no matter what PMI or PRINCE2 or any other BOK may say). If your client manages projects through Ouija boards and crayons, then so do you. We must learn to adapt and apply what we've learned as project managers to each client and each situation. As PMs, we should never force-feed. We must suggest, nurture, cajole—introduce slowly the project management concepts we know and love—and be enablers of success!

CHAPTER 7:
The Role of A Project Manager in Financial Services

Project management in financial services, as we are coming to realize, is extremely diverse in its definition, execution, and methods. This is also true for the role of project manager. Performing the role of project manager in our industry can involve everything from presenting to corporate CEOs to getting lunch for the company's office manager. The wide range of responsibilities the project manager takes on (or is assigned) are a function of the performing organization's culture and structure, business line and client base, and, perhaps most importantly, the personality and skillsets of the individual project manager.

When one looks to understand the role of project manager in financial services, one must again look at the culture of the firm in which that project manager works. The first question should be, "How does this company define project management?" (These methods are addressed in a previous chapter.) Many firms feel they are strong supporters of the discipline of project management because they have an enterprise license for Microsoft Project (see below). Other firms swing the pendulum the other way, by mandating that every project manager be PMP certified, attend thirty hours of training per year, and sponsor events and programs that further their project manager's education and training. Corporate structures and hierarchy also come into play when one looks to define "what is a project manager" in financial services. Is there a PMO? Are project managers employed in the individual business units, or are they used as a shared service out of a centralized group? The answers to these and a few other questions about basic organizational structure help us to understand what the project manager in each type of organization does on a daily basis, who the manager's key stakeholders are, where the manager's allegiances lie, and what the manager should expect from the organization.

We've all read what the Project Management Institute says about the three major type of organizational structures—Functional, Matrix (Weak, Balanced, and Strong) and Projectized. A summary is presented below:

Organizational Influences on Projects

Project \ Organizational Structure	Functional	Matrix			Projectized
		Weak Matrix	Balanced Matrix	Strong Matrix	
Project Manager's Authority	Little or None	Limited	Low to Moderate	Moderate to High	High to Almost Total
Resource Availaibility	Little or None	Limited	Low to Moderate	Moderate to High	High to Almost Total
Who Controls the Project Budget	Functional Manager	Functional Manager	Mixed	Project Manager	Project Manager
Project Manager's Role	Part-time	Part-time	Full-time	Full-time	Full-time
Project Management Administrative Staff	Part-time	Part-time	Part-time	Full-time	Full-time

2008 Project Management Institute A Guide To The Project Management Body of Knowledge - Fourth Edition

What we now need to examine is how this framework manifests itself in our industry in the form of daily tasks, responsibilities, and deliverables.

In a functional organizational structure, the role of the project manager most likely falls into that category found in every job description: "and other duties as assigned." First and foremost, the functional organization seeks to fulfill its daily operational responsibilities, and executing project work is a distant second. Project managers are most likely not trained as such, and are often assigned to "manage" projects after being handed a copy of the firm's project management methodology, maybe an installation of Microsoft Project, and a very high-level chat about what the project is about and when it has to be done. Very rarely will you see an operational group within a financial services organization stop and train its staff in project management (it does occur, but not regularly.) The projects, of course, usually only impact the department or unit in which they reside, and are therefore a natural fit with the subject matter expertise with which staff members come to the project. The in-depth content domain knowledge is what can make these projects successful, as the project managers will not only clearly understand the operational details of the department, but will immediately be accepted by the various stakeholders because of that knowledge. So, in fact, *the primary role of a project manager in a functionally constructed organization is that of subject matter expert.*

Matrix organizations start to add an expectation of project management discipline into their organizational models. As one move along the spectrum from Weak Matrix to Strong Matrix, it can be said that the role of project manager is taken more "seriously." Matrixed organizations, in project management terms, are firms where there are staff members focused entirely on project work. This occurs quite often in the financial services space, and is usually found in organizations in the beginning stages of evolution. The firm is beginning to realize that project work is becoming more of a daily factor in what they do, and are starting to assign "committed" resources to this work. Committed project resources, as we have come to learn, may take the form of either full-time employees (FTEs) of the firm, or contracted consultants. In a weak matrix, staff members may or may not be called project managers, and they may or may not receive formal training. Organizational support remains limited, with only slightly more access to any resources the project manager may need to complete a project. What changes here is often the span of the projects' impact on the firm as a whole. *Often a weak matrix structure evolves due to the fact that the organization is forced to define a method for coordinating projects that span multiple functional units.* It would not make any sense to set up individual teams in each department, so a cross-functional delivery model is defined. This project team will more than likely have at least a small percentage of their time officially "allocated" to the project, though normally that time is never subtracted from their commitment to their daily operational work. Still, a weak matrix structure offers subject matter experts a slightly better look at a more formal project structure, with probably the beginnings of what we'll later define as project administration. The primary role of the project manager here, however, remains content-focused.

As we move along the spectrum of project organizational models, our next stop is the Balanced Matrix organization. In this model, the company has at least defined the job "Project Manager" and has placed that role within one or more functional departments. At this point, the organization has acknowledged—at least at face value—the need for a more formal project delivery focus. The need to coordinate activities across multiple projects is again usually a driver here, but defining the more formal position of Project Manager is often in reaction to a company mandate of some type. As we discussed above, *project management as a function is sometimes more a requirement than a desire.* Internal or external auditors, as well as governing bodies such as the SEC, often require the ability to look back at how large client-affecting projects are executed at financial institutions. Project management is usually how they begin to assess the overall approach to these initiatives, as well as the ability for the executing firm to produce back-up documentation—business requirements, risk assessments, test plans—that quantifies the results and rationale for the project. This documentation is usually the by-product of a formal project management approach.

The Strong Matrix structure takes us one step further in defining the role of project management and project managers. In this model, there is a stand-alone department or group of project managers. This organization reports to the same management structure as its peer-level functional departments, but is engaged only in project work and is managed by what PMI terms a Manager of Project Managers. The project managers reporting to this group are responsible for coordinating the execution of projects for the overall management team, but report to and are evaluated by the Manager of Project Managers. Within this model, more formal project management practices, processes, and knowledge reside. Because this structure supports and nurtures project management as a discipline, it becomes a more attractive work environment for professional project managers, and therefore may become a project management center of excellence, where project managers can not only take advantage of the tools and methods available to them by the organization, but are afforded the opportunity to learn from each other. One side effect of this model, however, is that the pendulum of subject matter expertise versus project management expertise swings almost completely back toward the project management knowledge side. The fact that the project management group reports to the same company management as the functional areas supports an idea that some business knowledge should be available if needed from—or maybe even required of—project managers. However, the fact that a stand-alone department exists clearly makes evident that the organization values formal project management, and is willing to organize around it. The role of the project manager in this type of organizational structure now trends toward project leader. This model most commonly manifests itself in the form of a Project Management Organization (PMO). We'll explore the PMO and its role in a moment, but for the sake of discussion here we will define the PMO in terms of what PMI says—an organizational body or entity assigned various responsibilities related to the centralized and coordinated management of that project under its domain.[42] The PMO takes on responsibility for coordinating all of the projects within that group, company, division, or other entity.

The last organizational structure that PMI defines in the PMBOK is the projectized organization. In this structure, the vast majority of the work done is project work, and project managers truly have ownership and authority over their projects and resources. These firms have additional departments, such as Human Resources and Finance, but they primarily report in to the project group or provide support for projects. This model is most often seen in consulting organizations, whose entire business is based on project work. The project managers that work in such an organization are front and center in the overall business model of the firm, as successful projects directly correlate to revenue. The role of the project manager in the projectized organization goes beyond that of project leader and evolves into business manager. Projects in this type of structure are routinely the firm's direct income generators, so the project manager must not only know about the discipline of project management, but also be skilled in financial management as well.

Depending on the business line and industry sector, financial services organizations may employ all of the basic project organizations above. Large firms, in particular, will most likely be using multiple versions of functional, matrixed, and even projectized structures throughout their business lines. In departments that are high-volume processing areas, such as trade processing in custody banking or claims processing in insurance, functional structures are common. Here the department may only focus on small- to medium-scale initiatives to improve their operations, and these projects will probably be coordinated by members of the functional staff. They may or may not have project management training, but the limited size of the projects and their in-depth subject matter expertise will assist them with their project work.

Matrixed organizations are often found in medium to large departments or groups, where significant focus is put on the successful completion of projects. This is often the case in the investment division of a large mutual fund company, or the commercial lending area of a major retail bank. New product and service development and implementation are the keys for these types of businesses, and the ability to effectively manage projects that deliver these new ideas is paramount. Matrixed organizations, with their spectrum of subject matter and project management knowledge, are best suited to this business need.

Even the projectized organizational model can exist in a large financial institution. Companies that have stand-alone product or service sets that are implemented at or

---

[42] 2008 Project Management Institute. *A Guide To The Project Management Body of Knowledge,* Fourth Edition

delivered to clients (internal or external) often use the project management model. The perfect example is Bank of New York Mellon and their subsidiary Eagle Investment Systems. Eagle has a suite of software solutions, including data management, investment accounting, and performance measurement applications. BNY Mellon/Eagle sells this software to external clients, and then assists the clients in implementing the technology. These implementation projects are the majority of the work Eagle Professional Services does—the projectized organization of BNY Mellon.

As mentioned above, the existence of a PMO within the organization is a key determinant of the role of the project manager within a financial services firm. Not only may it be the internal department to which the manager reports, but by its very existence, it demonstrates that the company has made (and is making) a concerted effort to support project management and project managers. How the PMO defines itself, as well as its own internal mission and vision, however, will really be the driving force behind what the project manager does on a daily basis.

Beyond the straightforward PMI definition above, almost every PMO in every organization is different. Each defines its responsibilities in various ways based on the needs of the organization and the vision of the executives that lead them. Each of these responsibilities then defines the role a project manager fills within the PMO and within the overall organization.

As mentioned in a previous chapter, current thinking is that the responsibilities of the PMO include providing common methodology, vocabulary, knowledge, measurements and metrics, tools, process expertise, training, and development, as well as defining roles and responsibilities, assessing and auditing projects, supporting team development, assisting in project recovery, monitoring business performance and management, and guiding and mentoring project managers. In fulfilling these, the project manager alone must fill the individual roles of police officer, coach, thought leader, staff developer, and, of course, project manager.

Project Policeman is a role in which PMO project managers often find themselves. It is not especially glamorous or even fun, but, because of the position in which they've been placed, it is one of necessity. Project Police are in charge of enforcing the "laws" of project management that their organization has defined. The methods of enforcement vary, as do the "punishments" for non-compliance. Still, it is often the job of the PMO project manager to make sure that project methodologies are being used properly, deliverables are being produced appropriately, issues and risks are being tracked effectively, and so on. Depending on a manager's specific "jurisdiction," enforcement might be just within the manager's own project, across a department, or across the enterprise.

Project Policeman is a pure enforcement role. This role often exists where the PMO was created as a requirement for the organization. Often the most important responsibility of the project policeman is to make sure that the laws are being followed—but not necessarily to explain why they should be or how they can help a project. This again reinforces the idea of project management processes being executed because they've been mandated by an audit or a government regulation or a senior executive, not necessarily for business improvement. Being the project policeman is never enjoyable.

The role of Project Coach is taken on by a PMO project manager connected to another project manager in the organization who is charged with assisting the probably less experienced project manager in executing some or all of an assigned project. The coach's job almost entirely consists of ensuring that the project manager is enabled and empowered (remember that one?) to execute the project in a manner consistent with the PMO's and the organization's strategy. Project Coaches participate in everything from deliverables reviews to project plan development to communications planning. Project Coach can be a very rewarding role, but unfortunately is not very common because of tighter budgets and resource plans. Having an experienced project manager mentor another project manager as their primary responsibility may make perfect sense in the long term, but it can be a difficult sell to management that a very experienced project manager is just coaching another staff member, not actually managing projects.

Developing the role of Thought Leader within the PMO framework can add significant value to the organization as a whole, as well as offer personal and professional growth to the staff that participate in the process. The opportunities, however, to pursue this position—at least on a full-time basis—can be rare. Most financial services firms, whatever their sector, tend to focus almost exclusively on project execution, not philosophy (and rightly so). Project managers and project management continue to fight the war against being viewed as "overhead" on every initiative, so pursuing activities that appear to have little, if any, positive impact on a company's bottom line is not often very popular with senior management. Still, there are pockets of project managers creating new knowledge in our discipline from within financial services organizations.

So what is thought leadership and how is it being pursued within our industry? The quick definition of a thought leader is *an individual or firm that prospects, clients, referral sources, intermediaries, and even competitors recognize as one of the foremost authorities in selected areas of specialization, resulting in its being the go-to individual or organization for said expertise*[43]. For the most part, people look to be Thought Leaders

---

[43] Forbes.com http://www.forbes.com/sites/russprince/2012/03/16/what-is-a-thought-leader/

for one or both of two reasons: 1) they have something to say about a subject, or 2) they are looking to be recognized as an expert in a subject for reasons of self-promotion. Whatever the motivation, the current technology available in such communication venues as social media and self-publishing makes the physical availability of thought leadership channels easier to access than ever. There are thousands of project management blogs and websites, books (physical and ebooks), podcasts, and so on. What we need to factor in, however, are the very specific attributes of our industry, and how they can affect both a corporate and personal thought leadership strategy.

As we have mentioned, financial services, as a heavily regulated industry, is always looking over its shoulder. The industry as a whole is exceptionally protective of its any information related to operations, processes, and performance data —and again rightfully so. The confidence a client—any type of financial client—must have in a financial institution must be beyond question. Especially in large organizations, methods for sharing information or collaborating outside of one's one corporate function are rare—and, quite frankly, often discouraged. So to extrapolate this overarching philosophy across the ideology of thought leadership, is it really possible for corporate financial services employees to publicize new ideas and concepts they have discovered to the project management world at large? Again—mostly *no*. Most— and I say most—financial services firms strongly discourage, if not forbid, employees from blogging about their jobs or Facebooking about their professional lives. Many job interviews now are prefaced with the interviewer having Googled the candidate, looked at their Facebook or LinkedIn pages, or visited their website. Privacy laws aside, then, how can PMO project managers—or any financial services employee, really—let their project manager voices be heard?

There are a few ways that even the most corporate employee can look to further the discipline of project management through thought leadership. First off, there are quite a few firms that promote—either widely or not—the opportunity to publish and blog. Often these silos of thought leadership are standalone think tanks or R&D areas that exist for just that purpose: to come up with new ideas. Though you may not have the opportunity to spread your thoughts outside the corporation, at least you will be able to stretch your thought-leadership wings. Secondly, many smaller firms— especially software vendors or consulting firms—eagerly promote the opportunity to blog or in other ways publish new ideas or concepts in project management. Again, you would most likely have to have your name underneath the corporate header, but many firms have found out that creating new knowledge in their target client markets increases the company's exposure, and therefore increases business. And finally, you can just go do it – blog, write, speak, lead. Freedom of expression is a valuable attribute in society, and you will always find an audience for your new ideas in project management if they are well thought out and logical.

Staff Developer can also be a role for a project manager inside a PMO. Beyond just project manager coaching, the PMO project manager may have the opportunity not only to mentor a less experienced project manager in the execution of a particular project or projects, but also to advise the newer manager on career matters. More and more, organizations are setting up formal mentoring programs for project managers.

Of course, the most common role within the PMO is project manager itself. The primary responsibility of the majority of financial services PMO employees is to manage projects. The advantage here is that the project manager role in a PMO is usually supported by a strong infrastructure of tools, methods, and other resources. This often makes the role of a project manager in a PMO one of the better assignments a project manager can have.

Much of our discussion so far about the role of the project manager in financial services has been focused on what might be termed internal resources—i.e. project managers working on projects as full-time employees (FTEs) of the executing company. But there are other project management delivery models that employ different types of resources not directly employed by the delivery organization. These resources are project management consultants.

The role of Project Management Consultant is defined for our discussion as a resource brought in from an outside firm, or as an individual contractor, to manage a project or series of projects for a paying client. This role is very common in financial services firms because of the multitude of projects initiated by the industry and the frequent difficulty of hiring full-time employees to manage them. Often it is much easier to hire these temporary project managers to work for the firm for the length of the project, and then allow them to leave when the project is over. The temporary status of these resources will often "get around" the stringent head count constraints often found in both large and small financial firms.

The role of Project Management Consultant can be challenging even for the most seasoned and well-trained professional. In contrast to a full-time employee (FTE), a Project Management Consultant is—certainly at *some* level—viewed as an "outsider." The consultant often faces questions like "Why is this person here?" "Couldn't we do this on our own?" "Who does this person report to?" and of course "I bet they make a ton of money..."

A Project Management Consultant also must adjust to the client company in a different mode than one might as an incoming FTE. Where reporting relationships are usually somewhat defined for you as an employee, being a consultant often places you in between departments or groups or in organizational locales that may be quite murky—both to you and to your stakeholders. And where normally a project manager would have time to figure this all out while growing into a full-time job, a consultant is expected to be able to immediately operate at full efficiency from any-where in the organizational chart.

Project development also takes on a different approach as a Project Management Consultant. *Each project must be approached as though you are leaving the firm when the project is over,* because you most likely are. This perspective can end up having either a positive or negative influence on your performance as a consultant, depending how you process the situation. In positive terms, because the Project Management Consultant has no real internal allegiance to anything but the project (not the department, not the long-term growth of project management at that firm, not the company's political climate, not the stakeholder that may write your review), you are truly free to focus only on the success of that project. The other side of the coin is, of course, that you must be careful not to be perceived as having a total lack of project ownership.

Project execution in the role of Project Management Consultant also takes on nuances not always resident for an FTE. Client satisfaction, for a Project Management Consultant as for the rest of us, remains critical. What may be different is the way one considers it as a consultant, and how satisfying the client fits into one's overall project management persona. This may vary greatly depending on the employment status of the project manager. As an FTE, the "client" is most likely either the project sponsor or the actual end user of the ultimate project deliverable. However, to the Project Management Consultant, the "client" is most often the person that hired/contracted for the consultant's services. This may or may not be the sponsor or the eventual end client of your project deliverables (most often it's not). Because of this, the Project Management Consultant may approach the delivery of the project differently. For example: as an FTE, the project manager most often does not work directly for the "client." The client may be an internal "stakeholder" or perhaps an external customer of the firm for which you are employed. In this situation, the project manager's true success (as an FTE) may reside not with the success of the project, but with the success of the employer. The long-term *professional success of a Project Management Consultant, resides with the success of the client— not necessarily the success of the project.*

One additional project management role also common in the financial services industry is that of Software Vendor Project Manager. Our industry is run on technology, and technology is run on software—trading systems, accounting systems, imaging systems, and so on. The work involved in both developing and implementing these systems takes a very specialized form of project management. While the usual project lifecycle—Initiate, Plan, Execute, Control, Close—exists in most software implementation projects, there are several knowledge areas very specific to software vendor project management. These knowledge areas are Stakeholder, Product, Organizational, Industry, and Project Management Knowledge. Though these subjects sound very familiar, their application to software Vendor Project Management is unique.

Knowing your stakeholders in the Vendor Project Manager space is critical. All project management methods and approaches espouse the importance of stakeholder management, but in the world of the software vendor, constituencies are unique and often not understood. There are three major stakeholder groups involved in the implementation of a third-party software package:

1. External—Client
2. Internal—Project Team
3. Internal—Parent Organization

The Vendor Project Manager must manage all three groups effectively, but the manager must also understand that the interpretation of such standard project elements as objectives and success criteria will vary greatly across the three groups mentioned above. For example, the internal parent organization (where the Vendor Project Manager works) may view success in terms of profit, while the external client is focused on delivered functionality and the internal project team on timely delivery. The importance here for the Vendor Project Manager is to acknowledge the existence of the groups at project initiation, set the correct expectations in terms each finds important, and manage against those agreed-upon criteria.

There is a long-standing argument among project managers regarding the importance of subject matter expertise. One side of the argument says that in order to effectively manage a project in a complex domain like financial services, the project manager must possess very detailed subject matter expertise, even more than project management knowledge. The other side of the argument reverses the importance—it says that any strong project manager can manage any project, no matter the subject matter. In the role of Vendor Project Manager, there is little doubt that subject matter expertise—in this case deep understanding of the software product being implemented—is critical to success. Without that knowledge, the Vendor Project Manager faces the following challenges:

- Damaged perception with the client, as the client probably expects the project manager to be able to answer almost every software product question directly
- Delay in issue resolution, as the project manager must track down, understand and deliver the resolution back to the client

- Limited business and professional development, as without this in-depth knowledge, the project manager's parent organization is a little more challenged to sell that project manager's value to the client (and therefore the project manager's own standing within the organization can be put in question).

The importance of the Vendor Project Manager understanding how their own organization operates—both officially and unofficially—is often overlooked by project managers who are new to the software vendor space. However, the ability of the Vendor Project Manager's own company to respond to the manager's attempts to satisfy a client's expectations is often the greatest area of frustration for many a software implementation project manager. PMI does not teach us to assess, for example, how quickly one's software development group can code a fix for a "bug" discovered two days before your client is going "live." There's no section in the project manager's new employee handbook that describes how to find the one expert in your company with the knowledge of how to run the only report your client needs. Knowing the capacity of your organization to react to various types of issues—and how easy or hard it is to gain access to these solutions—is critical to the success of a Vendor Software Implementation Project Manager.

Industry knowledge, as we've mentioned several times, is very important to any project manager in financial services. It is not different in the Vendor Project Manager space—having a very thorough understanding of the industry will give a project manager immediate credence with the manager's clients and employing organization. Vendor-side project managers are expected to have the ability to not only implement the software provided by their company, but be able to provide guidance to the client on how that software will be optimized within their specific business model. Depending on the industry sector, software complexity, and business functions being addressed, this guidance might take the form of anything from a simple workflow change to a major strategic shift in how the client does business.

In the area of industry knowledge, though, breadth is more important than depth. This is because, more often than not, the Vendor Project Manager will have to work with many different clients using many different business models and approaches. Even if the manager's company services a very specific market and function, it has been illustrated that a diverse set of industry-specific experiences is more valuable because:

- No two companies are alike.
- Being able to offer a different way of doing things adds value to your clients. You need to have seen different ways to do this.

- Having a wider experience set allows you to be valuable to a wider set of potential customers within your industry, thereby adding value to you as an employee of your company.

One must remember, though, that often the business experience the Vendor Project Manager has gained is not always directly transferrable to project management or consulting. For example, if a project manager was a bond trader at a large asset management firm, the experience gained in executing trades would be highly valued by a vendor of bond-trading software only if the project manager was able to transfer that knowledge in a consultative manner to that vendor's clients. Now factor in the need for a project management skill set (see below), and you begin to see the challenge.

Last but definitely not least, a software vendor project manager must be an excellent project manager. That is not necessarily the same thing as "must have a thorough knowledge of project management processes" or "be PMP certified." Formal project management training is very important to this role, but it cannot take the place of some of the soft skills that are sometimes more genetically inherent in a good project manager. The three keys to maximizing the use of project management principles in a software vendor environment are:

1. Understanding the delivery organization's position on the role of a project manager—Depending on many different variables, software vendors consistently differ on the definition of the role of "project manager." It is critical to understand this up front in order to best prepare to manage all of your stakeholders (internal and client). For example:
    a. How is the role positioned during the sales process: As a process-based role? Total ownership of the project? Paired off with a client project manager?
    b. Is a project manager expected to also perform business analysis? Technical activities?
    c. What are the project manager's responsibilities internally? P&L? Billability?

2. Understanding the client's expectations and abilities around project management.
    a. Do they expect a certain level of product expertise?
    b. Will the client also have a project manager on the project? How will they interact?
    c. What is the level of "maturity" of the client's project manager and project management process?

3. Understanding how to employ good project management practices where there is little appetite for the perceived time or expense they may add to the project.
    a. How does one manage risks and issues when client budgets do not allow for formal processes?
    b. What are the absolute mandatory project artifacts, and what can be "lived without"?
    c. How and where do you draw the line between good project management and good fiscal practices? Do you ever?

The role of Software Vendor Project Manager is very unique. To be successful, one must be able to quickly learn the specific skills necessary to perform in that space, while at the same time hone one's existing project management expertise to fit in this role. It's just one of the many flavors of project management for us to try.

TIP: Project Management vs. Project Managers

In this financial services world of budget cuts and running "lean," one question that I have begun to ask my clients seems simplistic, but is the potential key to the most efficient and productive project management approach:

Do you need project mana-GERS or project manage-MENT?

If you think about it—good or bad—a lot of what we do as PMs are tasks. We report actuals versus estimates…we update issues lists…we publish plans…Of course we all know that project management is more about leadership and communication than being able to update an .mpp file. Still, in the business world in which we find ourselves, our economically challenged stakeholders are often unwilling to pay for what they view as "superfluous" (yes—a client did call project management superfluous) activity. What I propose is quite simple: Create a model where you identify the most critical activities that your organization must perform in the area of project management, then train all your capable employees (not just PMs) to execute them. This way, if stakeholders are hesitant to fund full-time project managers, your organization will still be in a position to deliver efficient and thoughtful project manage-MENT. Then, for projects that have the funding and need for more dedicated project mana-GERS, they, too, will be versant in the same tools and technologies that their organization has defined as PM requirements for all projects.

What I'm saying is: have your stakeholders focus on delivering project management—even if it has to be without project managers.

CHAPTER 8:
Stakeholder Management In Financial Services

Before going any further, let's spend a moment looking at stakeholders and stakeholder management in our industry. PMI defines these groups as persons or organizations (e.g. customers, sponsors, the performing organization, or the public) involved in a project or whose interests may be positively or negatively affected by the performance or completion of the project. Stakeholders may also exert influence over the project, its deliverables, and the reject team members.[44] What further defines stakeholders in financial services is the significant role played by corporate culture and organizational structure. How an organization (performing or client) operates on a daily basis demands special attention when determining one's stakeholder management strategy.

Let's first examine internal stakeholders—the persons or groups that a financial services project manager must work with within the manager's own organization. As mentioned in a previous chapter, the company for which one works creates—either accidentally or on purpose—the project management organizational structure and role expectations for each project. Whether at a functionally organized company expecting "accidental project management" or a fully projectized firm using mature processes and deliverables, a project manager in our industry usually goes into a project with

---

[44] Project Management Institute. *A Guide To The Project Management Body of Knowledge*, Fourth Edition (2008)

something of a predetermined set of guardrails (whether the manager is aware of them might be a different matter). What comes with this set of expectations are internal stakeholder groups that need to be addressed. Let's look at a few scenarios.

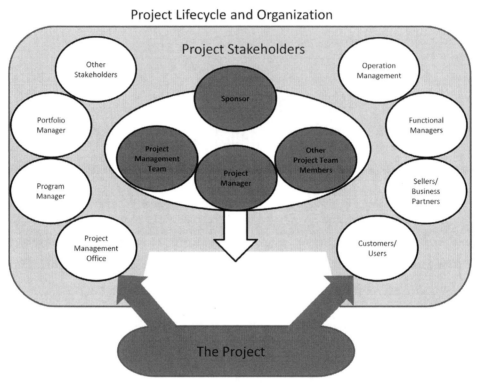

2008 Project Management Institute A Guide To The Project
Management Body of Knowledge - Fourth Edition

First let's take the functionally organized company. Odds are, the project manager assigned to this new project reports directly to the sponsor, who is most likely responsible for not only the success of this particular project, but the daily operations of the department most affected by the performance and deliverables of that project. This sponsor probably has very specific expectations around the project and the project manager. The sponsor will be focused on following the progress of the project deliverables, but also have some attention on the project manager. The project manager is probably not a full-time project manager and therefore may still have operational responsibilities that must be met. The sponsor may be monitoring whether the project manager's daily work is being impacted by this "project" stuff and may be more of a "nice to have." The flip side of this sponsor/project manager relationship is that the usual requirement of having to satisfy both the project sponsor *and* the project manager's reporting manager doesn't exist. Where sometimes the requirements and expectations of these two stakeholders may be at odds, in this case, this conflict does not exist. For example, a project manager in a matrixed organization might work for one manager, but have a different manager as the project sponsor. While the sponsor would most likely have the project objectives as a main focus, the reporting manager might have other duties in mind for the project manager outside the project manager role. The competing priorities in this type of reporting structure can often impede progress on both fronts.

Expanding the stakeholder circle out to the next level, the project team members are the next key group. Again, in a functional organization, the team will most likely be small and most likely not be full-time. *The key to managing this stakeholder group is to manage the team's time and expectations about the project and about project management in general.* The project team will most likely also be on the project as only a portion of their responsibilities, so understanding and empathy is important. They must know that the project manager understands the staffing model, and will also understand if they're pulled away. The project manager should call upon enough project management to enable the organization to fulfill its objectives without causing the project team to get bogged down in creating deliverables. It is also helpful to remember here that the project team members in a functional organization are most likely not used to working on project teams and within the project delivery model. It is up to the project manager to ensure that the team has the appropriate level of education and support as they mature along these lines.

The project team in a more matrixed environment within financial services may be a little more familiar with the project work paradigm, but it still most likely is not their full-time job. These stakeholders most likely have daily operational responsibilities, and probably view their project work as something that has to be done for now. Managing these resources is still about setting and supporting expectations around the team members' performance. Team members here need as much education on the essence of a project as they will need in completing their activities and deliverables. Similar to those team members in a functional organization, matrixed resources (with less need as the organization moves from a weak to a strong matrix) must be allowed to perform their daily "real jobs," and be expected to have priorities set for them that may not place the project first.

The project team members are managed a little differently in a projectized organization. Here project management gives way to more ***project leadership;*** being more experienced project resources, these stakeholders can usually be counted on to understand working within a project context. They key here is to take advantage of two-way feedback, as experienced team members will be able to offer solid ideas on project execution and strategy, where their less experienced functional counterparts may be stronger in subject matter expertise, but less experienced in project delivery.

Stakeholder management in financial services, once expanded beyond project teams and sponsors, becomes far more complex. As a project's context spans corporate and customer functions, the issue of communicating the appropriate message at the appropriate time to the appropriate audience becomes next to impossible. Communications planning becomes the key. This involves not just having a weekly status update meeting, but developing a deep understanding of the multiple stakeholder groups, the message each should receive, the medium through which they should receive it, and the timing and frequency of each message. This is your basic communications planning process, but the over-regulation, complexity, and culture of risk aversion in the financial services industry makes this often informal exercise critical. For example, in one project, one may have stakeholders interested in the performance of the process (PMO), performance of the project team (functional managers of team members), corporate governance (internal auditors), external governance (external auditors and internal compliance groups), performance of the project (sponsor), and finally the actual delivery and performance of the ultimate project deliverables (the customers!). Each group wants to know the status of their particular interests in the project. Some of this can be handled with standard communications like project status dashboards or meetings. Other communications—more ad hoc—also play a key role in stakeholder management of financial services projects. As we have come to know, financial services organizations as a whole spend a great deal of time planning for someone else to review their decisions. This is why *informal communication networks become essential.* One must anticipate every possible communication path for each information byte and ensure that no one is kept out of the loop. The "loop" is very important. The financial services industry suffers from widespread information paranoia, and any successful stakeholder management plan must be carefully prepared.

As a project manager in the financial services industry, the majority of your time is spent managing the stakeholders that are somehow part of the executing organization. Client stakeholder management, however—meaning actual customers—is also a key focus area. Much of the same analysis done for internal stakeholders must be done for external ones. Most clients with whom project managers will communicate are, of course, in the same industry and subject to much of the cultural pressure found within the performing company. The communications process, however, may be a little different. Often, the project manager is not the primary contact for the performing organization in the financial services industry. There may be client service representatives or salespeople that are the client's first contact. Once the project manager is introduced into the process, it is important that the manager and the external client develop their own communication channel in order to solidify the project as a standalone entity. When the project manager is identified as a primary contact, it is up now up to him or her to assess the necessary communication messages, channels, formality, and style of the communications that will be required to successfully execute the project. This might very greatly across the financial services project delivery model, depending on the role of the project manager. For example, if the project manager is part of a large financial software firm and the external clients are firms in which the manager is implementing that company's products, the project manager will have multiple communications objectives. The project manager is the primary face of the company, and therefore must represent the "company line" to clients. The manager also *may need to develop —through mutual trust—a more informal communication channel with their client contact(s).* This can be very important, when there need to be occasional "just between you and me" conversations that keep the project going. These may not be taught in the PMBOK, but, to experienced financial services project managers, theses "sidebars" often allow messages that would be difficult to get through formal channels the path that they need.

A different view of external client stakeholder management is necessary for the financial services Consultant Project Manager. To the Consultant Project Manager, the person who did the hiring is the external client. However, the Consultant Project Manager is often hired to execute a project *as a representative of the hiring firm*, so the clients of the firm are also the external clients of the Consultant Project Manager. This can be extremely complex. The project manager must be faithful to the execution of the project, the hirer (playing the roles of both sponsor and client), and the actual recipient of the project deliverables, who also could be looked upon as both the sponsor and the client. This situation arises fairly often (as project manager consultants are used widely in financial services) and is best handled through making a hard and fast differentiation between the two constituencies— the performing organization as the sponsor and the external client as the client. Also good to remember here is that the project manager consultant is in a unique position to focus attention primarily on the good of the project itself. The consultant does not have to worry about the internal political or organizational nuances of the performing firm—the consultant is there to do a job, and the rest should take care of itself.

We have seen that organizational and corporate cultures play a critical role in defining how a financial services project manager prepares and executes a stakeholder management strategy. The overarching societal attributes of the industry, coupled with the project execution maturity and success objectives of each stakeholder group, impacts the communications necessary to ensure the appropriate information is delivered in the proper format and timing to satisfy each constituency.

TIP: Managing Customer Expectations in Financial Services

Ron, the manager of the professional services team of a large financial software vendor, makes the following observations on the management of customers and their expectations: All too often project managers carry around with them the old cliché "The Customer is Always Right" to fall back on or obtain buy-in from other project team members when facing the type of customer who wants everything to work their way. In financial services, we are trained to make a good impression on the customer even when we know they are wrong. This must make some sense, since millions of people have spent time in these types of classes. So this becomes the logical scenario for any project manager to follow when developing their working relationship with their customers. During the early stages of the project, this principle becomes a very important way to gain credibility with your customers as you kick off and find out what scope and boundaries you now have to work within. But what happens when you are faced with a situation where the customer is not always right?

Especially in financial services, where strong personalities and egos are at the forefront, it is very easy for project managers to encounter customers who are straight up wrong, incorrect, or just talking from their backsides. This presents a unique challenge to the project manager, who now must carefully weigh the customer's desire against whether or not the project's goals and objectives will be negatively impacted. If they will not, then while remembering your allegiance to the project, you must swallow your pride and move on without disagreeing with the customer and stand behind the decision or course correction going forward.

However, if you feel strongly and disagree with the customer, then you must take caution before immediately expressing disagreement and creating a hostile perception that you are right and the customer is wrong. This will kill any goodwill and credibility you may have built up until that point and in most cases lead to your eventual downfall. This situation is where project managers should invoke the basic skill in customer service: make a good impression on the customer, or "MAGIC." Listen to the customer; play back your understanding of their point, request, or direction, making sure you are on the same page; and along the way, whether to take this away or engage now. As project managers, we have an obligation to respond to the customer, pointing out the tradeoffs the customer is now faced with regarding time, scope, or budget should you move ahead with them. This, at the very least, is the easiest way to show the customer how they must either align with the project goals and objectives or become a game-changer. If they have the authority to change the game, then you follow the change control process in place and everyone becomes aware. If not, then immediately document the customer's request, requirement, or position and then communicate up! There is an old cliché still around that says you should pick your battles, but project managers should replace that with "the customer may not always be right, but they are always the customer."

CHAPTER 9:
Managing The Triple Constraints: Cost

When one discusses project management in any industry, the famous "triple constraints" are always a popular topic. Actually, there are *four* triple constraints—cost, time, scope, and quality. How these constraints are managed and planned for in financial services again follows the familiar theme—a variety of methods firmly based on industry, sector, and culture.

Cost management in the world of financial services projects takes on many forms. Most industry sectors—large institutions, vendors, and consulting firms—do look to both plan for and manage the costs of their projects. The way they execute this, however, is distinctly based on their particular industry domain sector and their own organizational culture. Budgeting, or planning for, the cost of a project follows this pattern. On a granular level, how do financial institutions plan for the costs of a project? How do they decide to attempt a project in the first place? One process they follow is the development of the *business case*. This practice has been around the corporate world for quite some time, but is actually just becoming more common in the financial services project space. Now found both in larger institutions and in smaller, product-driven companies, taking the time to develop a full analysis of not just the project's financial components, but the market potential and the expected benefits from the project—both qualitative and quantitative—has always been and remains the basic approach most take to create an initial project budget. But the requirement of having a full-blown business case—and the approval process that it includes—is a recent addition to the financial services project management process.

As discussed, many large projects in the industry have been undertaken for the simple business rationale of a senior manager within the company coming into a meeting and simply stating, "wouldn't it be cool if…" And off we went. Recently, however, this project initiation process has changed, and for a couple of reasons. First off, the advent of the role of Business Project Manager has driven the more careful analysis and quantification of project benefits *before* any work is begun on the initiative. The Business Project Manager role evolved from the fact that most large projects in financial institutions were being run by the Information Technology departments. This was because, for the most part, IT was the biggest component of most large-scale financial services projects. Couple this with the fact that IT resources were probably more used to working in the project paradigm, and IT became the default project management department in large financial institutions. This began to change in the early 2000s, when business-side executives started to become focused on (and, quite frankly, paid for) realizing true business benefits from their product development and improvement initiatives. The business case also gained some traction because organizations were looking to identify efficient project prioritization and demand management methods through which the benefits of diverse project proposals could be judged equally. The business case, with its financial metrics such as Return on Investment and Internal Rate of Return, gave executives the beginning of such a method. It also became more popular as financial institutions soon began to implement a sanctioned corporate role entitled the *Business Project Manager*. The Business Project Manager was the person responsible for delivering the business benefits defined for an approved project. This was a purposeful departure from the legacy IT-centric project manager, who was initially responsible for all of the IT components of a project but became, often by default, the sole voice of project management for the initiative. This was due mostly to the fact that the business side often did not become involved again in the project—after approving the project and providing requirements—until user acceptance testing or implementation.

The Business Project Manager's responsibility begins when the project is just a nascent idea. It is the manager's responsibility to take that idea through the organization's project approval process, inclusive of creating a project proposal, developing the business case, and presenting the concept to senior management for funding approval. It then becomes the Business Project Manager's role to oversee the project from start to finish—actually beyond finish—and ensure that not only are IT activities being completed, but also all the other tasks required to make the project a business success.

This may include developing marketing plans, pricing and distribution strategies, sales forecasts and collateral, and any other peripheral activities that would make the product of this project a success. It is therefore the Business Project Manager's responsibility to manage the project's costs through its entire lifecycle. The manager can then track the costs back to the business case and make any adjustments necessary to continue to support the business initiative. The Business Project Manager role is most commonly used for new product development or improvement initiatives where there is an IT component as well as business activities, but it can be used in any project where multiple project stakeholders require business-focused oversight to ensure that overall business benefits are not overlooked during project execution.

Another common project cost-estimating process used in financial services is based on high-level top-down assessments of approximated deliverables. This approach employs staff representatives from the multiple internal stakeholder groups that may have worked on a particular project. Once these people have become familiar with the basic business objectives of a project—usually delivered in a summary document— it is their responsibility to estimate how much effort and associated cost would be required to complete the deliverables outlined in the summary document. This process is usually facilitated by the project manager, who then becomes the owner of this estimate as the project commences. The project manager usually combines all the estimates, constructs dependencies as accurately as possible, and presents the overall project estimate and schedule back to the initial participants for review and approval. Where this process can become complex is when some team members are not in agreement with the plan put together by the PM or their fellow participants. Because the various components of the plan (like the requirements phase, database work, or user acceptance testing) were estimated alone, the various dependencies of available resources and timing of deliverables could only be assumed as "best case scenarios" (examples like "we can develop the application code if we get the requirements on XXX date and can have "Sally" available to help out on the second Monday of every month"). Much additional work is often required to integrate the many different stand-alone estimates into a cohesive plan using the same set of project assumptions.

Other common methods of project cost estimating—often found within consulting firms and software vendors—involve using the results of previous projects to drive the initial estimate on a future one. This method usually takes the project budget from a completed project of similar size and scope as a starting point for the new project. Assessing the differences between the legacy project and the new, the project manager tweaks the cost estimates to be more in line with the anticipated scope of the new project. This adjusted estimate now becomes the budget for the new project.

All of the above-mentioned cost-estimating methods deliver to the financial services project manager the same result—the project budget. Depending on your organization and how the ongoing costs of a project are tracked, the operational project budget may take on many forms. It may be just one number against which the project manager will compare another number at the end of the project. The budget may also take the form of a set of project deliverables and associated cost estimates. Another form for a project budget may be a simple list of all of the people on the project team, a per-hour/month/year cost, and an estimate on the effort and associated total financial impact attributable to each resource. Whatever form the initial budget takes, it now becomes the responsibility of the project manager to track, manage, and communicate the progress of the project against that budget.

Projects Behind Schedule and Over Budget

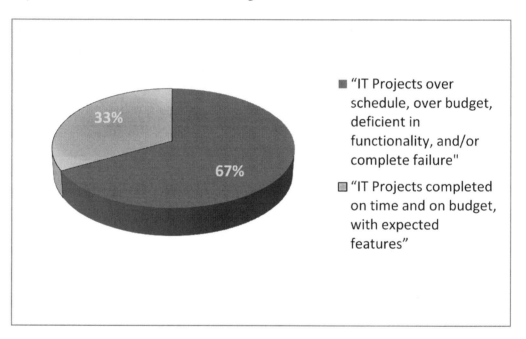

Source: The Standish Group Chaos Summary, 2006–2011

So what tools and techniques does the financial services project manager have to manage a budget? First off, there needs to be a process to track "actuals"—how much budget has been used to date. This is most often accomplished by having the resources working on the project enter their hours worked into some type of time-tracking system. Many such systems are available commercially, though some financial institutions have developed their own. The larger enterprise project management applications—like Microsoft Project Server and CA Clarity—have time entry functionality integrated into their systems. Whatever the system (often simply Microsoft Excel), these applications take the hours worked entered by the project team members, multiply that by the resource's hourly/monthly/annual pay rate, and gives the project manager the cost for that resource per the milestones or tracking parameters created (by resource, deliverable, or monthly burn rate, for example). Often these numbers are not available in real time, and have to be accessed on a periodic basis, like weekly or monthly. Whatever the reporting period or budget segregation, the project manager seeks to be consistently armed with updated financial information to assess the project's health.

The reality is that *most financial institutions track budget information but have a very difficult time using it to improve project performance*. This is simply because the firms rarely make a connection between the financial information being collected and the effectiveness of the work being done. In simplest terms, if you are 50 percent through your schedule and 50 percent through your budget, isn't it also important to know that you've only completed 25 percent of the work? This is the information that is missing from most financial services project cost management systems. This brings us to the concept of ***Earned Value***.

Earned Value is an approach where (usually) the project manager monitors the project plan, actual work, and work completed to see if a project is on track. Earned Value shows how much of the budget and time *should* have been spent, with regard to the amount of work done so far.[45] This metric would seem to make sense as a valuable means through which to continually assess one's project. Unfortunately, it has not truly caught on in the financial services sector for a few reasons: 1) Project scheduling estimates are seldom done at the detailed level required for effective earned value calculations. 2) Earned Value mandates that resources be assigned to activities for the actual number of hours/days that they are estimated to be on that project activity. Often project plans done in schedulers like Microsoft Projector are done at a summary task level, and frequently not resourced at a granular level. 3) Projects often involve multiple systems that are not connected or not optimized for this functionality. For example, a firm could be using CA Clarity for scheduling and a "home-grown" system for capturing hours worked, so there may be no way to integrate the data to calculate earned value.

For most organizations, furthermore, the time and effort it would take to apply earned value management principles and calculations just does not seem worth it. It is

---

[45] Duncan Haughey, PMP www.projectsmart.co.uk/what-is-earned-value.html,

also often the case that the way an organization allocates its internal project costs does not lend itself to capturing and reporting on detailed financial metrics. Internal costs are often not combined with external costs (vendor, consultants, and so forth), giving project managers only half the story.

Once a comparison of budget "actuals" versus estimates is captured, this information is shared through project communication channels and reviewed. Usually, it is a simple assessment of "are we under, over, or on budget" given where we should be in relation to timeline or deliverables. If a meaningful negative variance is noticed, the standard questions usually follow: What actions are necessary to remedy the situation? Is additional budget necessary? (Change control processes are addressed in a subsequent chapter.) How will it be allocated? Does the additional budget affect my original assumptions as far as the project's financial metrics? ROI? IRR?

One additional wrinkle is the fact that, although projects often go over the calendar year end, and can last for longer than twelve months, many large financial institutions still budget for projects on an annual basis exclusively. That means that projects that are not ready to start when the budget cycle is completed may be delayed. It also can mean that budget reporting often has to end at year end and start again in January.

As we have seen, project cost management processes, practices, and tools very greatly within the financial services space. A project manager may go from being asked to develop, present, and track a full-blown business line to simply having to capture the team's total hours worked at the end of the project—or anything in between. Even with all of the multiple processes and tools available and in use for project cost management, there still are consistent gaps in the ways financial project managers track project costs. The one most prevalent is the missing link between the project budget and the planned activity. Tying the two together is essential for capturing additional metrics like earned value. It remains common, however, that many potentially complementary project management processes—like cost/duration, effort/duration, and time/effort—are not used appropriately to take full advantage of their potential for improving execution. Still, cost management has come a long way in our industry. Most projects do capture and measure cost performance. What varies is the way financial institutions use that information to improve their business.

TIP: *Earned Value LITE*

John, a senior partner of a global strategy and technology consulting firm with over thirty years of experience in financial services and other industries, often recommends what he has termed *Earned Value Lite.*

Earned Value Lite (*EVL*) takes into account the financial services industry's less than consistent method of tracking costs by removing costs from the earned value equation. Instead, John has his team work with their clients to identify a series of finite milestones that must be delivered against throughout the lifecycle of the project. Each milestone must have associated with it a definite deliverable. As his team and client execute against this series of milestones, as each is completed (a milestone here is either complete or incomplete—Yes or No), it becomes part of the numerator of a very simple equation: Number of Completed Milestones divided by Number of Total Milestones = *EVL*. *EVL* is the true percentage complete of the project. In this scenario, project managers and team members are no longer responsible for calculating their estimated progress (what is 42 percent complete, anyway?). A realistic picture of the status of the scheduled work is quickly and easily presented and understood. John has used this approach in projects with budgets of tens of millions of dollars, and swears by its success.

CHAPTER 10:
Managing The Triple Constraints: Time

Time, or schedule, management practices in financial services projects are simply inconsistent. When we talk about schedule management here, we are addressing the processes and procedures that a financial services project manager uses to estimate, track progress, and adjust the duration of activities and tasks necessary to complete a project. Again, the corporate culture and industry sector greatly influence the process here. Some sectors of financial services are extremely good at schedule management because their livelihood depends on it. In other areas, however, managing the time and effort it takes to complete a WBS is looked upon as a purely administrative task, and pushed to the "back burner." This often causes much consternation later in the project when questions arise about the accuracy of the current delivery dates. Much like cost management, schedule management has evolved over the last decade, but in many organizations, it remains a practice that is ad hoc and in need of attention.

Schedule management starts, of course, with developing a project schedule. *This initial estimation process is one of the most inconsistent practices within the financial services project world.* Conventional wisdom says that the project manager creates a Work Breakdown Structure to define the work and deliverables to be created, then he/she identifies the activities required to complete those deliverables. After that, the time it will take to complete each activity is estimated. These tasks are then put in the correct sequence necessary to complete the deliverables, and the resources that will be required to do the same are outlined. Voila—the project manager now has a schedule, and, upon further examination and calculation, a project end date that is the best estimate at this point.

Unfortunately, adherence to conventional wisdom is inconsistent at best. After twenty-five years in the financial services industry, this author can honestly say that he has never seen, nor had the opportunity to use, a Work Breakdown Structure to plan or estimate a project. The few attempts to do so were met with much resistance or doubt. It is just not a process or tool that has gained acceptance.

Duration estimation within financial services projects is usually done from a "top-down" perspective. "Top-down," or starting at high-level/summarized activities (or even a project end date) to estimate the duration of other similar activities is normally a process used when the firm has done several projects of a similar type. Because the company has a good idea how long this type of project will take, it has the confidence to estimate the duration (and deliverables and resources) of the new project, taking into account any differences between the completed projects and the new. Although this application of the "top-down" model is used in financial services, it is most often found in other "projectized" organizations where there is a substantial history of completed (successful and unsuccessful) projects on which to base the new project's estimation. This estimating process, however, is consistently found in financial services organizations organized all across the project organizational model.

"Top-down" estimation is usually done within the financial services industry because the project manager has been given a mandatory delivery date. This, of course, is not exclusive to financial services—many industries use this approach to manage projects. Unfortunately, this less-than-optimal practice is often the basis for the estimated duration of many projects.

A better estimation method, "bottom-up," should be used for project types that may be unfamiliar to the project manager or the organization. It follows something of the same path as the WBS-based process above. In the "bottom-up" process, major project deliverables are defined, and then the detailed activities necessary to create them are identified and estimated. Then these activities are sequenced and resourced, giving the project manager a project-level estimate. The reason that this method is more appropriate for unfamiliar projects is that it forces the organization to think through the actual work that would be involved and roll that up into a duration estimate.

Often available to help us out are project management tools capable of using many different types of estimating models to produce a duration estimate and schedule.

Microsoft Project is one; others include Oracle's Primavera P6 and CA Clarity. Depending on the application and the skill of the user, these tools can be extremely helpful in developing realistic estimates. What can happen, though, is that these tools will suddenly appear to take on a mystical power that either strongly repels or attracts believers. A project scheduler will only deliver output based on your input.

Once an original project duration estimate is created and communicated, the next significant hurdle the financial services project manager must overcome is the universal misunderstanding of the word "estimate." The simple fact that every project manager has come to accept is that *stakeholders believe that the milestone dates put forth on the first day of the project will never change through the last day of the project.* No amount of rationalizing will ever change that fact. Not that this should change the way a project manager manages a project—it is just a plain hard truth that project managers must learn to manage.

If a project manager has to constantly explain the meaning of "estimate," it often helps to explain the terms "progressive elaboration" and "sliding window of project management" as well. Progressive elaboration is defined as "continuously improving and detailing a plan as more detailed and specific information and more accurate estimates become available, and thereby producing more accurate and complete plans that result from the successive iterations of the planning process."[46] This is an important concept to stress with your stakeholders, who think that the project manager has all of the information necessary at the beginning of the project to tell exactly when the project will end. The same stakeholder education process should be done with the idea of the *Sliding Planning Window of Project Management.* Also known as the *Rolling Wave,* the Sliding Planning Window is based on the premise that you should only plan in detail as far ahead as is sensible at the time. Often project managers are asked to plan a project in minute detail from beginning to end, hoping to eliminate uncertainty. This isn't possible. A detailed plan takes a lot of time and effort to develop and maintain. A plan that is too detailed too far ahead will simply consume resources and become inflexible.[47] Whatever rationale one might use, it is very important that financial services project managers stress that fact that **there is no such thing as an exact estimate.**

Once the initial estimate is complete and the project is underway, it is now the responsibility of the project manager to manage the schedule. The activities that a financial institution includes in managing the schedule, of course, vary from firm to

---

[46] Project Management Institute. *A Guide To The Project Management Body of Knowledge,* Fourth Edition (2008)

[47] http://www.jiscinfonet.ac.uk/infokits/project-management/sliding-planning-window

firm, but most involve several common factors: time tracking, percentage of work complete, and change control.

Time tracking—capturing and reporting the actual minutes (hours, days, months) spent working on a project—is a very common practice for financial services firms looking for metrics to gauge the progress and status of their projects. The methods and tools used to capture the time worked are very similar to (and in fact often done as part of) the capture of project costs. Many commercially available systems applications will capture hours spent by time period, deliverable, activity, or any of a number of options. Home-grown systems continue to exist as well. Again, analogous to the process discussed in cost tracking, project resources are asked to enter the time they worked on a specific project into the time tracking system in terms of hours, days, or months.

What does differ between organizations, however, are the milestones or "buckets" used to capture and segregate the time. For example, some organizations have project staff track their time against specific project activities. Resources access these activities from the project plan, and post their time against the tasks on which they worked. Other firms have their people track time against a specific project deliverable or phase. The team members will identify the high-level phase—such as Requirements Development—and post their time against the phase, no matter which Requirements Development activity they worked on. Still a third time-tracking methodology involves the staff documenting their time against a specific time period. These folks will post the number of hours they worked in a day, week, or month to a specific *project*, without having to specify what actual activities they worked on.

There are other approaches. Some organizations will have only IT resources track hours against a project, never factoring any time spent by the "business" team members and their effort on the project. There are also firms that only track the effort of consultants or "external" resources, without assigning any measurements to the time spent by their internal staff.

One additional time-tracking nuance that does deserve mention during this discussion is the difference between tracking (and estimating) effort and duration. As project managers, we all know the inherent difference. Effort is the physical working time necessary to do something—for example, to write this code it will take forty hours of work. Duration is the calendar time it will take—using the same example, if two people work on this task it will take them twenty hours (duration) to do this forty-hour (effort) task. Conventional wisdom says that a project manager should be tracking both, as they are directly related. In practice, however, the relationship is somewhat bifurcated. As mentioned, project team members are often asked to post the time they worked to specific (or general) project activities on which they worked. Sometimes these activities will have estimates specifically for them; sometimes they will not. If these tasks or deliverables *do* have a time estimated for them, most likely it will be a *duration* estimate, not one based on effort. *Most often in financial services, duration is used for estimating time, effort for cost.* Unfortunately, seldom are they as connected as they should be. As mentioned in the chapter on cost management, most often cost (budget) and time tracking are done in different systems. This is primarily because *the level of detail used in defining project tasks is not fine enough to allocate true effort, resulting in ineffective use of scheduling and time-tracking systems.* Let's take a look at this.

As mentioned in a previous chapter, the most commonly used estimating methodology is "top-down." What this gives you is high-level effort and duration estimates for either the project as a whole or several major milestones or deliverables. Now the project manager must assign resources to these high-level activities, such as "Develop User Interface." Unfortunately, there are probably several dozen tasks that go into developing a user interface, but those haven't been defined yet. All the project manager has to work with is a single task that has been scheduled for fifteen business days of duration. On the project are three developers assigned to developing the user interface. But the project manager does not know exactly what each developer will need to do or when, so the manager simply assigns all three to the task. Now the project scheduler will process this as three developers on a fifteen-day task, requiring five days of effort from each. *The system will also reduce the duration of the task to five days.* For communication purposes, the project manager needs the plan to show that the activity lasts fifteen days, so that either the developers' allocation to the task can be adjusted to 33 percent per person, or the activity can be extended to include fifteen days of effort for each developer. Now one can see how easily the effort and duration metrics can get out of synch, and also some of the disadvantages of "Top Down" estimating and tracking.

As mentioned above, time and schedule management in financial services really takes two tracks—the time capture and management piece is part of the cost/budget management process. This involves the tracking of actual hours and associated costs discussed in the previous chapter. The schedule management aspect, as illustrated, is different and separate from time and cost tracking in financial services. Schedule management is simply focused on delivery dates.

The management of milestone and delivery dates in financial services is as much about the management of expectations as it is about data and deliverables. As mentioned previously, setting a delivery date in financial services is as close to "carving it in stone" as one can get post–new millennium. This is due to many factors, both cultural and tactical. From a cultural perspective, *financial services organizations revolve around certainty*—or at least the perception of certainty. Black and white. One dollar equals one dollar. Three days to settle a trade. If the amounts match, the trade settles—if not, it doesn't. Checking accounts have enough money to cover a check, or you overdraw. *Projects revolve around uncertainty*—especially in the early stages. Things change. This is why financial services stakeholders hear the project manager identify a potential project end date, but do not hear the fifteen or sixteen caveats in the sentence immediately following. The stakeholders crave certainty. This, of course, creates a major disconnect between industry culture and project reality.

Tactical realities also impact the ability of financial services stakeholders to accept the concept of an estimated delivery date. As we've talked about, much of the overall management of financial organizations is done within a series of "time boxes"—budgets are set annually, projects are approved at defined intervals (mostly annually), bonuses are fixed and paid annually. Because of this, the management process in these companies needs a finite time frame for project execution so that the projects can fit into the existing management model. There again is a mismatch between the industry culture and project management process.

There is one sector of our industry that does a very good job of integrating the time-tracking process and the actual performance of their projects—the professional services/vendor side of financial services. Whether it's a software vendor, large multinational consulting firm, or single contract project manager, the vendor "side" is much better at equating the effort and duration measurements of a project to how the project is being executed—because they have to. These firms often bill their clients by the hour and are asked to justify the work they've done. It is of the utmost importance for vendors to both estimate and track time and cost accurately, because it is their livelihood.

So how does one manage the project schedule for a financial services project? Much of the answer to that depends on how "success" has been defined for the project, and what metrics are in place to monitor that definition. Extreme caution must be taken in almost every scenario when setting expectations around delivery dates. Our industry is extremely focused on that final end date, and every deviance from that magic day will be monitored and questioned throughout the life of a project.

Communications planning is critical. There needs to be a very well-defined communications channel for disseminating schedule information. Often, financial services stakeholders do not want any delivery date different from the original estimated date disseminated unless they have approved that change. Change management and control (we will discuss that in the next chapter) is also an important aspect of managing the schedule. There needs to be an agreed-upon process for identifying major changes in assumptions and their impact on the schedule (and there also needs to be an agreed-upon definition of "major changes".)

From the perspective of tracking time, it is very important at the beginning of a project to understand both the organization's and the project team's expectations for how and why their project effort is going to be captured. Often different groups within the same company will have different policies and procedures for time tracking, and those internal practices may supersede any parameters the project manager may plan on utilizing in the project. This is often the case in functionalized or weak matrixed organizations, where departmental polices come first. Also, the use of the data captured from time tracking should be clearly defined. Why are we capturing hours or days worked? If we have used 50 percent of the allocated budget, are we 50 percent complete? What if only 25 percent of the work is done? Ease of process use is important—again, especially if the project manager is working with a less experienced project team. Define time-tracking systems that capture enough data without causing excessive additional work. Make it as easy as possible, unless the performing organization demands scheduling minutia.

As with many project management practices, corporate culture and structure have a great deal of impact on how scheduling and time is managed in financial services. There are various methods of defining the activities or deliverables against which time should be managed, as well as the process to manage them. Estimating the duration and effort of a project is also approached differently in different organizations—"Top Down" in most, "Bottom Up" occasionally. Whatever the method, *seldom will one run across a financial institution that doesn't whole-heartedly believe that the first estimate of a delivery date is the final estimate of the delivery date.* Though all of this, the project manager must be clear in setting expectations. Team members and stakeholders alike must be clear on what elements of schedule management will be utilized—time tracking, change management, and so on—and how and when information will be communicated. It is through this communication process that all project stakeholders will stay informed.

TIP: Microsoft Project is Smarter than You

There, I said it. We've all thought it, or at least thought that Microsoft thought it: MS Project truly is better at your job than you are. How many of you project managers out there have ever typed a "finish" date (or start date, or…) into the appropriate column in MSP only to hit "Enter" and have the date simply not change? You type it in again, and the date does not change! Of course the omnipotent MSP is just enforcing good project management practices in one way or another. Thank goodness! Maybe you have a dependency that does not allow that activity to finish on that date, maybe the resources you assigned cannot complete the activity on that date, or maybe you did not offer sacrifice to the Gods of the Gantt Chart view. For whatever reason (and believe me, MSP will have a good one), you are being forced to use correct scheduling protocol. You may not want to, but you can't argue with an application—especially one that probably got a better score than you on the PMP exam…

CHAPTER 11:
Managing The Triple Constraints: Scope

P roject scope management, according to our colleagues at the Project Management Institute, includes the processes required to ensure that a project includes all the work required, and only the work required, to complete the project successfully. Managing the project scope is primarily concerned with defining and controlling what is and is not included in the project.[48] The steps for achieving successful scope management are further defined as Collect Requirements, Define Scope, Create WBS, Verify Scope and Control Scope.[49] Within the financial services project approach, this process—at a high level—is traditionally followed. Where our industry begins to have trouble is finding the appropriate level of detail at the start of the project, and in our expectations of the state at which requirements can be turned into the next phase of the project.

As the start of any project, there may be varying degrees of scope definition. In some cases, full business cases may have been written, with detailed business requirements defined as part of the overall rationale for the project. In other cases, there simply may be the one-sentence scope statement "Wouldn't it be cool if…" Whatever the case, the scope definition available is usually captured in an initiating document

---

[48] Project Management Institute. *A Guide To The Project Management Body of Knowledge,* Fourth Edition (2008)
[49] Ibid.

such as a charter or an initiation report. This becomes your baseline high-level project scope.

Following this initiating document, detailed business requirements are gathered from internal and external stakeholders to further define the project's scope. Most project management practices in our industry—the waterfall approaches, certainly— desire to have close to 100 percent of the business requirements defined during this first phase. The sign-off and approval of these requirements becomes the scope verification, and now the project is ready for the next phase of execution (as mentioned in a previous chapter, the use here of a Work Breakdown Structure is extremely rare). Any potential scope alteration after the approval of the business requirements is addressed through change control.

Now, our old friend conventional wisdom would dictate that it would be nearly impossible to be able to identify every aspect of the required project scope up front. Just as we mentioned the constant of change in the discussions of cost and time management, scope change is also an expected component throughout a project's lifecycle. Projects often experience an evolving clarity of requirements, where the further along in the project's lifecycle one travels, the clearer the detailed requirements become. Unfortunately, financial services have a difficult time planning for evolving requirements, as their project methodologies often demand final requirements as a mandatory early-stage gate to proceeding with the project. There are methodologies, such as Agile development, that are based on accepting changing business needs, but by and large, financial projects look to define and approve all requirements as soon as possible.

A change control process is undertaken when a change in cost, time, or scope is identified by one or more stakeholders of a project, and the component that may be changed has been approved or baselined. The details of the change control process vary from organization to organization, but the basics remain the same. The potential change is captured on a change request form; then the change is assessed by all the appropriate parties as to its true impact on the project in terms of cost, time, and scope. Once all of this information is documented, the change request form is submitted to the change control board or project sponsor for review. If agreed upon, the change requested will be used to update the budget, schedule, and scope statements, and a new baseline will be set. Where the financial services industry is often challenged is in weighing the often substantial overhead one must accept to process a change request when not using an Agile approach. This idea of Agile has a business representative embedded with the rest of the project team. When an idea for a change to the project comes up, the business owner reviews its impact, and immediately the project moves again. Given what we know about the industry, it should be no surprise that having that much unsupervised autonomy is very rare. But it does exist.

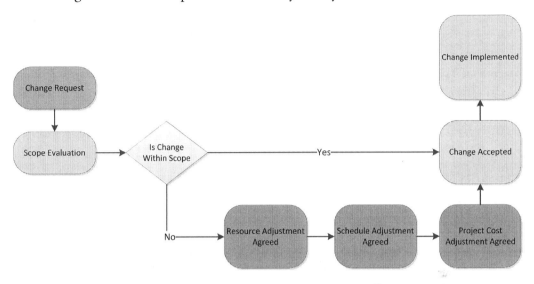

Typical Scope Change Control Process[50]

The major issue in terms of scope management in financial services projects is also very common throughout the entire project management world. This is the infamous "scope creep"— the idea that project scope often expands slowly and almost covertly. This creeping has the habit of affecting the other two of the triple constraints—cost and time—directly, without these additional areas of scope ever really being addressed directly. *The reason much scope creep occurs is that project managers often expect too much from their initial scope definition and too little from their project's ability to absorb change.* We've mentioned several times our industry's cultural attribute of always anticipating that the work you do will be reviewed. That concept nurtures the idea of striving for perfection, and waiting until you're sure you have it before you act. When you translate this approach to defining requirements for a project, it is in direct conflict with the fact that things change. Ideas change. Technologies change. People change. What occurs in the standard financial services model is that the requirements-gathering time is extended in an attempt to capture every possible project requirement up front. Once these requirements are approved by the stakeholders, the perception is created that everything the project will ever be required to deliver has been documented and approved. As we know, this is never the case. However, because we've built the idea

---

[50] Assisted Evolution http://www.assistedevolution.com/ae/en/services/project/changecontrol.aspx

that that the team has captured everything, having to eventually *change* these require-ments, and therefore the scope of the project, becomes almost foreign. This breeds the sometimes elaborate (and costly) change control or change management processes that many large financial institutions have introduced. These firms have built such high expectations around their original scope estimates that having to change them becomes a project unto itself.

The other aspect of scope management that financial services project managers tend to overlook is their project's inherent ability to absorb a good amount of change within the boundaries already set at the start of the project. This is primarily due to the project estimation processes used by our industry. As mentioned above, much of the overall estimation done for projects within financial services is from a "Top Down" approach. This model, by definition, bases much of its rationale for cost, time, and scope estimates on high-level deliverables and milestones, with much detail underneath those milestones missing. Therefore, these estimates will have very little direct connection to the detailed requirements being gathered, and any changes being made to those as the project moves along. It is very difficult, then, to assess the quan-titative impact of any "change" if very little had been originally quantified. Taking this one step further, because the original estimates are less directly connected to individual requirements, there most likely is significant "float" already in these num-bers. When project managers or stakeholders place too much credence in the original estimates in this scenario, they assume that any proposed change must be added (or subtracted) directly from those estimates. Assessing the impact of change in this situ-ation is extremely difficult.

Much of the process of managing project scope in financial services projects is driven by the organization's philosophy on managing change. If the firm focuses on gathering all requirements at the very beginning of the project so scope can be "locked down," then scope management becomes a controlled process of approvals, change requests, updates, and more approvals. This has been the most common approach in the industry, and often is the best fit with the check-review-check culture of financial services. Estimating processes also impact the scope management approach, as it is often difficult to assess the impact of the addition or deletion of scope items if the project has not been estimated at the same level as the scope items. Overall, scope management in financial services projects is about setting the correct expectations with your stakeholders around how and when scope will be defined and through what process it can be changed. If all stakeholders are on the same page, then the dreaded "scope creep" should be greatly minimized.

TIP: The Sticky Note WBS

I had the opportunity to interview another financial services project management veteran:

Dave is a PM with over fifteen years of experience within the insurance and securities industries. One thing we started to talk about was the practical use of the Work Breakdown Structure in financial services projects. While we both agreed that the WBS is always spoken of in project management circles as a critical tool in planning the scope of a project, neither of us had seen widespread use of it during our own project delivery experience. We discussed the possible reasons for this, and just came to the conclusion that the effort required to explain, construct, and manage the WBS was usually viewed by stakeholders as more project "overhead." Still, Dave had a way of using the important output derived from the WBS—project scope.

After Dave had initial conversations with his stakeholders about project scope and approach, he would go back to his office and begin to construct a classic WBS using "sticky" notes. Dave would go through, at his desk, the basic decomposition of deliverables and note each on a separate "sticky note," until a full WBS for the project would begin to take shape. This final configuration would then be shared with his stakeholders in the form of either a scope statement or the beginnings of a project plan.

While we've all probably done similar exercises in meetings with the active participationof our stakeholders, Dave's approach is unique in that it not only accepts, but plans for, the "pushback" an industry project manager may experience while using important PM tools not necessarily familiar to team members with more operational backgrounds. Instead of potentially expending energy on endlessly explaining the merit of such methods, Dave has come up with a personal variation on a common meeting exercise and uses it to his advantage. The resulting outputs save valuable time and deliver the value of a possible more traditional WBS.

CHAPTER 12:

The Fourth of the Triple Constraints: Quality

Traditional project management discussions have, for a long time, focused on the "Triple Constraints"—cost, time, and scope. Over the last several years, however, a fourth component has been added to this triangle—quality management. Going once again to our friend the PMBOK, quality management ensures that a project will "satisfy the needs for which it was undertaken," not just meet or exceed the requirements. The PMBOK Guide also says that quality is the degree to which a set of inherent characteristics fulfill requirements.[51] In terms of how this might manifest itself in a financial services project, *quality management is about ensuring both the quality of the project management process as well as the quality of the product produced.*

The quality of the project management *process* is often overlooked during execution. Process quality might take the form of ensuring that the methodology is followed efficiently, that the project deliverables are in good form, or that the stakeholders are satisfied. It is not necessarily focused on product quality, though product quality should be an offshoot. Process quality is usually only managed or addressed by financial institutions that have something of a mature project management process. These are most likely strong matrix organizations or projectized firms. The most common vehicles for process quality management are deliverables and "lessons learned" reviews.

---

[51] Project Management Institute. *A Guide To The Project Management Body of Knowledge,* Fourth Edition (2008)

Deliverables reviews can be conducted as part of the sign-off and approval process for any major project deliverables, whether they are documents, plans, or software code. Input should be received for these reviews from all affected project stakeholders and customers. Each deliverable is assessed across a set of metrics specific for that item. For example, the User Acceptance Testing Plan might be looked at in terms of inadequate test cases coverage, incorrect or missing test cases, documentation and typographical errors, automation errors, build issues, exception and error handling, environment issues, or nonconformance to process standards. The requirements documentation process might be reviewed for incorrect or missing functionality, incorrect or missing non-functional requirements, incorrect or missing user interface, incorrect or missing system interface, nonconformance to process standards, or documentation/typographical errors. The important thing to remember here is that the review is being conducted in terms of the quality of the process—not necessarily the quality of the product being produced. Here, we focus on form and context over content.

Lessons Learned reviews are normally held at the conclusion of a project (though they can occur before), and focus on reviewing the results of the project, the project management process, what went well overall, and what did not. A typical list of Lessons Learned topics is presented below:

Project Lessons Learned Review

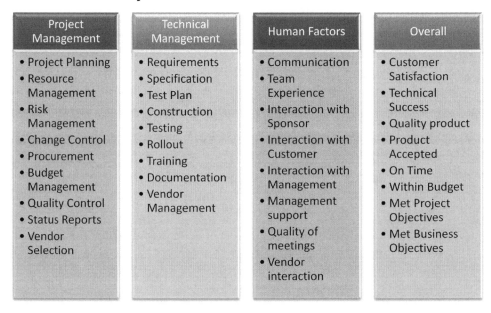

Project Management	Technical Management	Human Factors	Overall
• Project Planning	• Requirements	• Communication	• Customer Satisfaction
• Resource Management	• Specification	• Team Experience	• Technical Success
• Risk Management	• Test Plan	• Interaction with Sponsor	• Quality product
• Change Control	• Construction	• Interaction with Customer	• Product Accepted
• Procurement	• Testing	• Interaction with Management	• On Time
• Budget Management	• Rollout	• Management support	• Within Budget
• Quality Control	• Training	• Quality of meetings	• Met Project Objectives
• Status Reports	• Documentation	• Vendor interaction	• Met Business Objectives
• Vendor Selection	• Vendor Management		

Project ManagerTips.net — Grantham University

Although it is a fairly common practice to hold Lessons Learned reviews in the financial services industry, *what is often missing is a process through which the lessons are actually assimilated into the overall project management model of the organization*. What is needed is a formal methodology step, executed during the estimation phase of a project, where project managers are required to view an organizational database of lessons learned to assess if there is any knowledge to be leveraged from an old project to the new. This is the best way to truly take advantage of the results of Lessons Learned.

Moving on to the quality of the product produced by a project, two main areas in our PMBOK address managing that process—Quality Assurance and Quality Control. The method through which these areas are managed is:

Plan Quality—the process of identifying quality requirements or standards for the project or product, and documenting how the project will demonstrate compliance

Perform Quality Assurance—the process of auditing the quality requirements and the results from quality control measurements to ensure that appropriate quality standards and operational definitions are used

Perform Quality Control—the process of monitoring and recording results of executing the quality activities to assess performance and recommend necessary changes.[52]

Although project or process quality is sometimes mentioned, most activity around quality management in financial services projects is centered around Product Quality, with the primary focus (certainly in the IT space) on software testing.

Current research shows that 30 percent[53] of all time and cost associated with the development and implementation of software is spent on testing (5 percent unit testing, 15 percent integration testing, and 10 percent acceptance testing). This testing, which would be classified under the Quality Control heading in the PMBOK, can be further broken down into the following processes:[54]

- *Unit Testing*—A series of stand-alone tests are conducted during unit testing. Each test examines an individual component that is new or has been modified. A unit test is also called a module test because it tests the individual units of code that compose the application.
- *System Testing*—System testing tests all components and modules that are new, changed, affected by a change, or needed to form the complete application.

---

[52] Project Management Institute. *A Guide To The Project Management Body of Knowledge*, Fourth Edition (2008)

[53] Knowledge Structures Inc . http://www.ksinc.com/itpmcptools/EstimatingGuidelines.pdf

[54] John E. Bentley, *Software Testing Fundamentals—Concepts, Roles, and Terminology*. Wachovia Bank, Charlotte NC

The system test may require involvement of other systems, but this should be minimized as much as possible to reduce the risk of externally-induced problems.

- *Integration Testing*—Integration testing examines all the components and modules that are new, changed, affected by a change, or needed to form a complete system. Where system testing tries to minimize outside factors, integration testing requires involvement of other systems and interfaces with other applications, including those owned by an outside vendor, external partners, or the customer.

- *User Acceptance Testing*—User acceptance testing is also called beta testing, application testing, and end-user testing. It is where testing moves from the hands of the IT department into those of the business users. By the time UAT is ready to start, the IT staff has resolved in one way or another all the defects they identified. Despite their best efforts, though, they probably haven't found all the flaws in the application. A general rule of thumb is that no matter how bulletproof an application seems when it goes into UAT, a user somewhere can still find a sequence of commands that will produce an error.

- *Production Verification Testing*—Production verification testing is a final opportunity to determine if the software is ready for release. Its purpose is to simulate the production cutover as closely as possible and for a period of time simulate real business activity. As a sort of full dress rehearsal, it should identify anomalies or unexpected changes to existing processes introduced by the new application

Quality Control on most financial services projects follows the above-mentioned series of steps to inspect developed code. For the most part, IT resources perform the vast majority of the testing duties, including unit, system, integration, and regression testing. Methods of measuring success, as well as the level of automation, vary in the industry. And, of course, this testing lifecycle assumes a waterfall development approach. Where Agile methods have been deployed, testing is much more integrated into the development process, and is less a stand-alone initiative. Tracking the results of the testing (and "fixing") process is often less than completely transparent. Often internal (or external) development organizations—unless fully allocated to a specific project—have a somewhat ad hoc method of testing for software "bugs." This is because most "shared services" IT groups must split their time between fixing "bugs," developing new software for new products, and developing software to support legacy systems or products. The time allocated to "fixing" software issues in a particular project manager's product may be at the mercy of the developer's manager.

Software Testing and Cost of Defects[55]

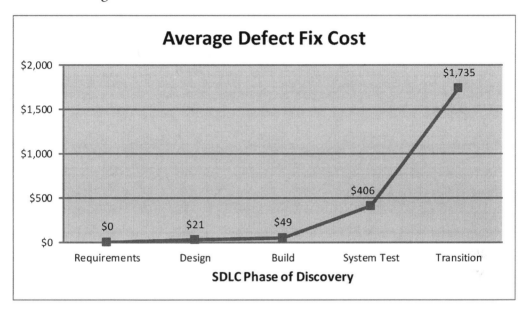

User Acceptance Testing – UAT – is most often the testing battleground in Financial Services projects. Up to that point in the project lifecycle– in the majority of projects – the IT department has been running the show (unless an Agile methodology is in use, but that is rare). They usually are responsible for much of the lifecycle from system requirements through integration testing, and have most likely only called upon the "users" intermittently (after the business requirements phase) for the occasional question or clarification. UAT is where the users should be ready to start to assume ownership of the testing. Unfortunately, in most organizations, business users are substantially less experienced in project work than most IT staff, and, most likely, are assigned to a project on a part-time basis. Therefore, *the project manager in a financial services project must plan for a substantial learning curve in the transition from integration testing to UAT.* This education process may involve initial or advanced training in the new software; the concepts of software testing; the planning, creation, and execution of test scripts; and the process for identifying and resolving software "bugs." Successful UAT is important to any project for a couple of reasons: first, it is the most rigorous and broadest testing that will be done to the application or

---

[55] Dwight Lamppert, Senior Test Manager, Franklin Templeton, Software Test Professionals Conference, San Diego, CA 2013 http://www.stpcon.com/Item/1064/,

platform, so functionally it is here where the most issues will be uncovered (and have to be resolved). Second, and probably more importantly, it is in UAT that the people that will be actually using the software get their greatest (if not their first) exposure to the application. UAT can be viewed as the true "proving ground."

When it comes to the management of quality in financial services projects, the focus remains on the traditional aspects of quality assurance and quality control. Planning for and executing these processes traditionally revolves around process quality and product quality, and product quality does receive more attention. Although financial services projects do execute such traditional process quality practices as lessons-learned and deliverables reviews, the process of quality control—inspecting for defects in the end product—remains the cornerstone of project quality efforts. Financial services projects usually work through the major phases of testing—especially on software projects—but are often challenged when it comes to user acceptance testing. The lack of experience by the users in project work, coupled with their often limited amount of exposure to the new software prior to the UAT testing, can make it a challenge to efficiently test a new application. Still, it is essential that the users participate in this process, as they will be the final judges of the functionality of the software and deliver the ultimate verdict on the project quality management.

TIP: You're the "U" in UAT

A good friend of mine was working on a large technology initiative at her current employer—a global investment and custody management firm with thousands of employees and operations all over the world. They were finished with the majority of development and design, and were now planning the transition from the point where the new technology was a "project" to where it became "the system." Of course, this transition involved a great deal of preparation, testing, and training, including User Acceptance Testing (UAT). Traditionally, UAT occurs at the point in a project where the current/future business users of the application or technology assume ownership of the testing and truly begin to assimilate (at least conceptually) its functions into their operations. (I say traditionally, because it is often very difficult to engage internal business owners in large projects where their participation up to this point has been minimal. The typical participation of business staff in a large-scale technology initiative—whether it be full-lifecycle development, system implementation, or some mutation thereof—is at the beginning (kick-off and requirements) and at the end (UAT and Implementation). This is not the case, of course, for some methodologies (such as Agile) that require participation throughout the lifecycle. What I've found, however, is that for most large-enterprise technology initiatives in financial services, old-school waterfall still applies: business people are involved up front…then at the end. But back to our story…)

My friend told me that after the business team went through a fairly rigorous exercise of defining potential user test cases and developing—with her guidance—an overall test plan (entrance and exit criteria, issue resolution, and so on), they would not formally approve the plan. *The business team would not formally approve the plan that they had actually developed themselves.* But why? Why would the team put in all that work and not be comfortable documenting their readiness to proceed?

On the surface, we hypothesized that it was simply fear…organizational fear that if the team signed off on a plan and then turned out to have missed a key element, they would have to shoulder any blame for any misfortune that occurred. This, of course, is very common in our industry. Financial services is known for supporting an "audit" mentality, where operations are run with the assumption that someone somewhere is looking over your shoulder. Whether this is appropriate or not can be discussed, but it is the truth.

So was it simple fear? We thought about it more. Yes, it was fear, but ***fear of the unknown***. This fear was not of making a mistake—it was general uncertainty around what the new technology truly did, and, more importantly, how their jobs and lives would change. The business team was not ready to assume responsibility for testing the system because they were not ready to fully accept the technology into their corporate lives. They had only (marginally, as I was told) been involved in the beginning of the project when requirements were being gathered. After that, aside from the occasional meeting or question, the business team was barely involved in the project at all. When it came time to formally test and accept the system, the business team received little training, and was expected to fully embrace the new technology. More importantly, they had been called upon to assess what functionality needed to be tested, how it was to be tested, what results they should expect, and what criteria they should use to either sign off as to the system being usable as their own or reject the new technology. No wonder this group was hesitant to put their name(s) down in digital ink!

So, how to avoid this situation?

1. Ensure the eventual users of any technology are involved throughout the life-cycle of that system's development/implementation. We have all heard it before, but unless the business users/clients/customers feel involved (and are MADE to feel involved) as the project unfolds, it will become much more difficult to transition formal ownership of that technology to these people when the time comes. The users need to be comfortable with the systems *before* they are asked to test and accept them.

2. Enforce the philosophy of ***"You're the U in UAT!"*** with your user stakeholders. This was a phrase I came up with many years ago when first addressing the problem of limited business user involvement during the testing phase of a project. It very succinctly captures for your business stakeholders that they own the final testing and acceptance of the system. We project folk can help them by suggesting approaches, tools, formats—but the testing content and eventual sign-off is a business user function.

3. Understand that this transition period does exist, and act accordingly. We, as project managers, must realize that there will be uncomfortable moments as our users, who may not have been engaged through much of the project to date, now come to the table. Many questions—some insightful, some not—will be asked, suggestions will be made, and confusion will be displayed as these people begin to understand the long-term impacts of the system they may have only heard about. We must be patient.

Transitioning a new technology from the project team to the eventual business owners can be tough. The trick is to get and keep these eventual users engaged in the beginning, middle, and end of the project.

CHAPTER 13:

Risk Management in Financial Services Projects

R isk management is an extremely hot topic in the world of financial services. With the financial crisis of 2008 still fresh in everyone's mind, the management of risk has become the number one priority in our industry. The new report from IDC Financial Insights predicts that risk technology spending across the banking, capital markets, and insurance sectors will reach over $74 billion by 2015, outpacing the growth of overall IT spending in financial services and comprising 15 percent of total IT spending in financial services in 2012. In addition, the introduction of new regulations coming from the Dodd-Frank Act, Basel III, and Solvency II are collectively inducing an outpouring of technology spending from companies in the financial services sector.[56] Risk management in financial services projects, therefore, is a vibrant area of focus, though often inconsistent in its practices and approach.

Project risk management has two components—the aspects of risk associated with the project itself, and the risk associated with the product produced by the project. As far as project risk management, the project manager here is responsible for anticipating, identifying, and mitigating the risks associated with the completion of the project

---

[56] Chartis Research's "RiskTech100," Sixth Edition

activities. Various methodologies are used to accomplish that, but the basic approach involves:[57]

1. ***Plan Risk Management***—The key output of this process is a risk management plan.

2. ***Identify Risk***—The key output of this process is a risk register.

3. ***Perform Qualitative Risk Analysis***—The key output of this process is a risk register update. This process analyses the probability, impact and exposure of the identified risk.

4. ***Perform Quantitative Risk Analysis***—The key output of this process is a risk register update. This process analyzes the financial impact of the risks on the project due to deviation from project objectives.

5. ***Plan Risk Response***—The key outputs of this process are the risk register update, risk-related contract decision, and project management plan update. Risk register update has the list of identified contingency, mitigation plans, and approach for responding to negative and positive risks.

6. ***Monitor and Control Risks***—The key outputs of this process are the risk register update, change request, and project management plan update. While performing this process can identify new risks, revisit the strategies for responding to negative and positive risks.

While the process above, along with a few others, is often attempted in the financial services project space, the issue that continually arises is not about the methodology through which risk management is begun—it is the inconsistency through which the practice occurs throughout a complete project's lifecycle. Projects in financial services—whether they be internal to large organizations or vendor/client initiatives—often pursue a rigorous exercise of identifying a comprehensive list of potential risks that might occur as the project unfolds. (quick definition: A risk is an event which may or may not happen, and if it happens, there will be a positive or negative impact on the project. The probability of the event happening is more than 0 percent and less than 100 percent. A project risk can also be an opportunity.[58]) Frequently, project teams receive additional training in risk management and are able to create a robust strategy for managing the various risk types, such as

---

[57] Project Management Institute. *A Guide To The Project Management Body of Knowledge*, Fourth Edition (2008)

[58] Ibid.

business, human resource, external dependencies, technical, or business case. Each individual risk is then reviewed along the prescribed method, and the most critical risks (resulting from the quantitative and qualitative ranking processes) are assigned a response in the Risk Management Plan. These responses are usually prescribed along a standard track:

- Avoid the risk —Action taken so risk has no impact.
- Mitigate the risk—Lessen the probability or impact.
- Accept the risk—Low probability or unavoidable. Changes to cost, schedule, quality or scope are acceptable.
- Transfer the risk—Transfer of risk to a third party, like a vendor.

In addition, risk triggers are identified as a means for alerting the project manager to a risk that is about to occur and preparing the manager to initiate the response. In looking at the six-step PMI risk management process, financial services projects usually perform steps 1–5 very well. Unfortunately, when it comes to monitoring and controlling project risk, financial services projects are not as proficient.

It is fairly common that project managers in financial services perform a risk assessment, formulate a risk management plan, possibly even schedule regular risk reviews, and include all of this information in the project charter for sponsor approval and sign-off. Most of the time, however, any formal approach to project risk management ends there. Perhaps it's because risks by definition are *potential* events—not actual things that have occurred—that financial services project managers find it difficult to "get their arms around" examining risks on a regular basis. As mentioned in a previous chapter, the culture of financial services firms is to support and reward *reactive solutions to emergent events*—the "firefighter" or "hero" mentality. *Resolving emergencies is valued more than avoiding them.* Because project risk management is, by definition, a process to plan for the avoidance or mitigation of emergent events, it is in direct opposition to the financial services corporate culture. *Project risk management is inconsistent in financial services projects because it's based on anticipation, not reaction.*

An additional aspect of project risk management is assessing the potential impact if and when a risk occurs. This is somewhat similar to estimating the impact of a change control request, where all involved stakeholders review the potential financial and technical impact to the project and assign dollar and time elements to the change request. In a risk assessment, the potential impact of the risk occurring is captured, as well as the probability it will occur. That impact, expressed in money and time, is often captured in an estimating "bucket" called "contingency" and added to the project pan and budget. This is a common practice. Of course, whether the risks occur or not, that time and budget usually gets consumed anyway.

Financial services project management also addresses what we term product risk. This risk management process, for clarification, does not look to assess the potential market risk of a product. In other words, product risk management in this case addresses the risks involved in the end product of a project potentially not delivering benefits. It does not address how an investment product might perform under various economic conditions.

In product risk management, much of the onus for evaluating and anticipating the risks associated with the final project deliverables resides more in the business rationale—or business case—than with the project team. Product risks, almost by definition, occur once this deliverable is produced. Risks here may involve questions around the product's adoption rate, ability to function within customers' environments, and overall profitability. For projects undertaken to improve or support internal functionality, there are product risks around the ability of that deliverable to produce the internal benefits—cost reduction, improved speed or automation, regulatory compliance—that the product was envisioned to deliver. Most product risks are defined appropriately during the design or definition phases of a project. This may occur in the project proposal and approval phase, during the development of the business case, or during requirements gathering. In a traditional Waterfall approach, the occurrence of the risk may not be predictable at all before the completion—or near completion—of the project. This, of course, is a tremendous risk in itself. Depending on the duration of the project—i.e. the distance between the time the product's benefits are defined and when they are delivered—the risk that either the environment has changed or the delivered product has changed through the life of the project grows. Using a more iterative methodology, such as Agile, can reduce this risk, as it may deliver products in smaller increments and sooner to potential clients to review or purchase. The downside here, of course, is that the fully functioning end product may not be finalized for some time, and also may be difficult to envision.

In reviewing risk management practices in financial services projects, it is important to separate the concepts of project risk and product risk. Project risk management focuses on the potential positive or negative events that could impact the execution of the defined project management processes and activities. The approach to practice in the financial services project manager world is fairly consistent—most firms have a defined methodology for identifying and planning for the potential occurrence of risks. Where many financial firms "fall short" is in their practice of executing risk management procedures *during* the entire lifecycle of a project. Organizations often identify the obvious and potentially impactful risks during their chartering or initiation phases, but fail to undergo the same exercise throughout the project in terms of having similar risk identification and planning sessions throughout the duration. This can lead to unpleasant surprises.

Product risk management—the process of managing the risks of the project's end product not delivering its defined benefits—often follows a different path. This process usually identifies the potential risks—often through defining expected benefits in a business case or initiating document—and then looks to confirm their delivery when the product is complete. Unfortunately, business conditions may have changed during the project's duration, so waiting until project completion—as in a traditional Waterfall approach—can itself be risky. Newer methodologies—such as Agile—address this by delivering products in smaller and quicker increments. This approach has inherent risks as well, but may be one answer to improving the overall approach to product risk management in financial services projects.

TIP: Reducing Risk by Improving Internal Team Expertise

Having spent well over two decades in and around the delivery of projects in the financial services industry, one can imagine that I have heard almost every argument, explanation, and viewpoint on what is the most important skill necessary to ensure project success—subject matter expertise or project management knowledge?

What I've discovered over the years is very simple:

1. Every project requires its own specific level of domain AND project management knowledge.

2. This level should be defined, adjusted, and reviewed (at least at a high level) before, during, and after project execution.

3. The delivery of this knowledge does not have to be by one person (or two, or three).

Depending on the organization, complexity, sector, and deliverables of your project, the level of expectation that the project manager will directly contribute to the content of the project will vary greatly. That, however, does not affect the actual amount of content necessary for the project to be successful. Often, organizations look to the PM to also be the subject matter expert. This becomes more and more difficult as the project becomes more complex. There may also be a direct correlation between the complexity of the project and the need for greater project management knowledge. And, as we all know, finding expert project managers with expert levels of subject matter expertise can be extremely difficult…and expensive.

So what to do?

Put together a team whose combined experiences sum to the level of project management and business knowledge you feel is necessary for the project.

Sounds so simple, right…but does anyone really try to do it? Who really takes the time to assess the level of subject matter expertise required for a project, understand the project management experience necessary for successful execution, and choose resources to fit those profiles? And—here's the important part—then empowers these resources to fulfill the roles as defined? This hardly ever happens…but is highly effective when it does!

CHAPTER 14:
Career Pathing For Financial Services Project Managers

P ursuing a career as a project manager within the financial services industry offers a person the opportunity to work on a multitude of different project types, complexities, and durations within many and varying organizational models. Within the industry, there are also various career paths a person might take, depending on their own personal objectives. In this chapter, we will look at some of the professional paths down which a project manager might travel.

Two distinct options for career paths for project managers in financial services are corporate employee and consultant. A corporate project manager in financial services might work for a large bank, investment firm, insurance company, or any financial institution not involved primarily in developing and implementing technology or delivering consulting services. The manager is a full-time employee (not a contractor) of the organization The role of the corporate project manager can be very rewarding, as the opportunity to work on complex, large-scale, and strategic projects increases because the nature of the organization. There is also the opportunity to work with a large variety of people on various teams, and, most probably, the chance to experience many of the different project organizational models (functional, matrix, etc.), as more established firms tend to have better-defined organizational models and supporting processes.

From a professional development perspective, the corporate project manager also has several options that may not exist in other career paths. Most organizations provide project management training and education for their employees at little to no cost to them (though recent budget cuts have impacted this). Even in a functional organization focused on daily operations, a project manager's chance of efficiently gaining more knowledge, either in project management topics or business subjects, is much greater as a corporate employee. Mentoring opportunities may also be available to a corporate employee, as well as tuition reimbursement to pursue an academic degree or professional certification.

There are also professional safety-net issues that a full-time corporate position often addresses. Financially, many people view being a full-time employee of an organization as more secure. They do not have to worry (in theory) about how many hours they have worked, whether they can afford to take a day off (if they have remaining vacation days!) or whether they will have a job at the end of their current project. Being a full-time employee of a firm also often allows the person to take advantage of paid (partially or fully) benefits such as health care, retirement plans like a 401(k) or pension, and paid time off. There is no need to look for new projects every six months or so (as you might as a consultant) or have to constantly prepare for and attend interviews. There is perceived safety in being a corporate project manager.

Project management as a practice has very specific attributes for a corporate project manager. One important factor is that there is a very good chance that the majority of a project's stakeholders—including the sponsor—will work for the same company as the project manager. This can be a great advantage to a project manager's project, as relationships should be based on a shared understanding of business objectives and corporate culture. Terminology will be familiar to all, as well as the tools, systems, and processes that the project manager and team will be using. As a corporate project manager, there should never be a question as to where your professional allegiance—or that of the team—should lie. It resides with the company that has employed you as the corporate project manager.

There are also, of course, areas that people might see as disadvantages to being a corporate project manager. Being employed by a single organization may not give one the opportunity to experience diversity in the way organizations are managed, the business that they conduct, or the culture that they develop and support. A corporate financial services project manager is most often given little choice as to which projects to work on or when to work on them. The same can be said about the teams with which they work—a corporate project manager is mostly assigned to a team with little say over the resources they can access. Corporate project managers must work on what is assigned to them by the company for which they work.

Financially, one is limited in growth when employed as a corporate project manager. Most firms have compensation boundaries tied to organizational levels, titles, and job grades. The actual money a project manager (or any employee) can make can be driven as much by their title as their performance. Growth in financial compensation is also constrained by the allocation of "raises" across the company and how the project manager ranked on an annual performance review. Depending on the methodology of the performance assessment process, it is possible that the project manager's supervisor has had little direct work experience with that project manager. If the company's performance review process does not allow for feedback from project stakeholders and participants, *the corporate project manager may again be bound financially by organizational, not project, measures of success.*

Professional development and educational opportunities may be more affordable with the backing of a large institution, but much of that has changed over the last several years. Programs paid for by one's employer are a lot fewer—if at all existent—in the post-2008 financial services industry. Not only is reimbursement less frequent, the subject matter and venues have changed dramatically as well. It is no longer common for employees to travel to seminars fully paid by their employer. Virtual and low-cost tools—like webinars and online classes—are now used to cut down on expenses. While these certainly improve the company's bottom line, the educational experience is somewhat reduced, as is potentially the employees' feeling that company values their professional development.

Project execution and delivery as a corporate financial services project manager can also be viewed as limiting. As a corporate project manager, you are most likely mandated to use a certain methodology and toolset—even if these may not seem appropriate given your experience. Your sponsor and stakeholders, while all employees of the same organization, may have entirely different agendas that focus more on internal political motives than on project success. Corporate project managers are often torn in defining their own—and often their stakeholders'—allegiances on the project. Who is the true client? If the project manager "reports" to one manager, but is beholden to another as project sponsor, which one is to be satisfied if both cannot be? And what if an external client is involved? For the corporate project manager, non-tactical (that is, organizational and political) factors play a very large role.

There are, of course, other career paths available for a project manager interested in the financial services industry. One of those is to become a consultant. Many types of consulting models exist, but here we will divide project manager consultants into two genres: firm-based and independent.

Firm-based project manager consultants are full-time employees of consulting firms. For further clarification, these project managers are assigned projects by these firms, and are not "contractors" who are always expected to leave the firm once a project is complete. The project work for a firm-based consultant can be very rewarding, in that they often have the chance to work on a variety of project types for a variety of clients. Depending on the firm, a firm-based project manager may on one project be defining the global strategy for a multi-national fund company, and on the next be defining the requirements for a general ledger accounting system. Firm-based project managers also are usually fortunate in being able to work with focused individuals who have chosen consulting as a career and are therefore experienced in both the project work and the consulting mind-set.

Firm-based consultants also have many of the "pluses" defined for a corporate project manager. Project managers here most likely have opportunity to pursue numerous professional development options (many consulting firms use this as a draw for employees), and are valued more when they do so. This has as much to do with the value they bring to the organization as with corporate interest in developing each employee. If a firm's consultants are better educated—both formally and informally—they become much easier to sell to clients. This is a win-win for both employee and employer, and a very attractive component in deciding to become a firm-based project manager consultant.

Many of the perceived "safety" factors are present for the firm-based project manager consultant as well. As an employee, one is not overly concerned with the direction from which the next paycheck will come upon project completion. Health care and other standard benefits are usually provided on a par with the corporate project manager model, as are paid vacations and holidays.

From a compensation perspective, salaries are usually a little higher for a consultant project manager. One reason is that there is a general expectation of a different required skillset for a consultant project manager than for a corporate project manager. Consultant project managers are expected to be incredibly flexible in their ability to execute projects because of the diversity of clients upon which they will work. That is not to say that corporate project managers are not as flexible, but for consultants it is a requirement. Another required skillset is the ability to "face off" on a daily basis with external clients and understand what that entails. This is not a skill a project manager can learn in school or through PMI—this is something born out of both tactical experience and personal and professional development. It is not easy to learn to understand and communicate the multitude of messages and interactions that occur between a consultant and client. Again, allegiances become an area where careful navigation is critical. Firm-based consultants have an allegiance to their firm, the client, and the project, as well as to themselves. The relationship between these allegiances is difficult to understand at times. Where does one place one's priorities when all four stakeholder groups are of different opinions on the same subject? The ability to answer these questions is difficult to train into a person—it's almost a natural talent with which one is born. It's this type of talent that is necessary to be a successful consultant, and that's another reason why they may receive higher compensation.

Higher salaries may also be used to compensate for the travel requirements that often come with the role of firm-based consultant. It is not uncommon for organizations to expect a project manager consultant to travel up to 100 percent of the time when assigned to a project. This can be a plus or a minus, depending on the person's desire to travel. Either way, it is assumed that these consultants do have the potential requirement of travel; the compensation for that is higher salaries.

From a project execution perspective, there is often a significant advantage to being a firm-based consultant. Many firms—especially those that specialize in project management in one form or another—have a very well-defined and well-performing project management process. After all, that is one reason a client would hire a consulting firm—they have better project management processes, tools, and methods. Because this is often the case, a project manager usually has a great opportunity to learn a great deal from the consulting firm and gain an improved skillset. In return, the project manager can also be afforded the opportunity to contribute new ideas to the knowledgebase of the firm. This interaction is often another primary reason for becoming a firm-based project manager consultant.

There are, as with any career choice, attributes of the firm-based project manager consultant role that some would consider disadvantages. Projects are still assigned to the project manager with little to no input from that person. This can even include being assigned a less–than-optimal travel schedule. As mentioned above, expectations around a firm-based project manager consultant's willingness to travel, in many organizations, is almost without question—i.e. the project manager goes where and when the firm says to go. If unprepared (or unwilling), this can lead to a high level of job dissatisfaction. Project responsibilities—whether based on existing skillsets or not—are often thrust upon a consultant project manager to satisfy an existing or future client. Project managers may be forced to play the role of subject matter expert in a subject where they have no expertise. This can make them very uncomfortable, and gets back to the somewhat inherent nature of consulting capability—people either have it, or do not.

Project management consulting is not for project managers who require consistency in their work environment. A firm-based project manager consultant is always starting new projects for new clients, always meeting new people and having to perform in varying corporate cultures and environments. This is not easy for everyone. In addition, it is often the added responsibility of firm-based project manager consultants to develop business—either with their currently assigned client or through other sales channels. This, again, is usually not in the job description of a corporate project manager, and may not be an aspect of the job that all project managers find attractive.

Still a third career track for project managers in financial services is the independent consultant project manager. The independent consultant project manager is defined as a project manager who is hired directly by a client firm or a staff augmentation firm (placement or "temporary" firm) to work on a project for a defined period of time. Once that period of time is over, the independent consultant project manager is no longer employed by the client or placement firm, and must find a new project on their own (or with the help of the placement firm). Being an independent consultant project manager is not for everyone.

The fact that one has to often find a "new job"—i.e. new project—every six months or so can easily scare people away. Still, for those that enjoy the challenge, it can be a very satisfying and rewarding (professionally and financially) career.

One of the major advantages of becoming an independent consultant project manager is that you have almost *total control of the projects on which you work, and the people with whom you work.* Please notice the word "almost." There are, of course economic factors to consider, and if there are few opportunities out there, an independent consultant project manager may have to take on a project that may not be ideal. But, in theory, an independent consultant project manager can turn down any project or any organization that is not attractive. The constant exposure to new organizations, new business models, new corporate cultures, and new people is similar to that of the firm-based consultant project manager. So is the requirement to possess exceptional consulting skills—maybe even more so here, as the independent consultant project manager has no organization to turn to for support in case of mistakes. The independent consultant project manager also serves as their own sales, marketing, HR and finance departments. This can give the independent consultant project manager a great feeling of independence…or dread.

An independent consultant project manager is usually well paid. The compensation, however, usually comes at an hourly rate (though many staff augmentation firms have taken to paying their independent consultant project managers on salary for the length of the project), and requires a little translation to be able to compare to what one would make as a firm-based consultant project manager. A common equation might be *Hourly Rate × 40 hours/week × 48 weeks* (accounts for holidays and non-paid vacation) – *Cost of Benefits* (must be paid by independent consultant project manager, though sometimes available through the staff augmentation firm) = *Annual Equivalent Salary*. The bottom line usually nets out to a little more than one might make as a firm-based consultant project manager. That difference is what this author terms the **Consulting Risk Premium (CRP).** The CRP is what a consultant gets paid to take the risk of having to look for a new job every six months or so. Back in the 1990s, when independent consulting became very popular, independent consultant project managers could almost work just nine months and make the same take-home salary as a FTE in one year. The CRP was high. These were the days of preparing for such unavoidable events as Y2K and the introduction of the Euro currency. The downturn in the labor market caused by the tragedy of 9/11 and the financial meltdown of 2008, however, has introduced a glut of qualified project managers into the independent consultant market because there is nowhere else for them to work. This has subsequently brought the available compensation for independent consultant project managers down significantly, thereby negatively affecting the CRP. To date, there is still probably a small financial incentive for project managers to become independent consultants, but no more than that.

The role of independent consultant project manager becomes even more interesting in the professional allegiances they have to interpret and actively manage. The independent consultant project manager most likely has the standard project sponsor and team members with whom to interact, but from there, relationships become exponentially more complex. The independent consultant project manager was probably hired or contracted by a team member in the organization, PMO or project management leader, or even the project sponsor. This "hiring manager" is the default client for the independent consultant project manager—the first person that must be satisfied. Or is it? If the project sponsor is not the "hiring manager," difficult choices may occur if the priorities of the sponsor are different than the priorities of the "hiring manager." What is best for the project—in the opinion of the project manager—also must be a consideration. What is often inherently unnecessary for the independent consultant project manager is any need to consider the long-term corporate political or cultural impact of any project decision. This can be a major advantage of the independent consultant role. Independent consultant project managers are there purely to worry about the project, not the politics. This is a welcome environmental change to many who have made the transition from corporate to independent consultant project manager.

One other significant advantage of the independent consultant role is that you often have the opportunity to truly add to the project management processes and practices of the organization at which you are contracting. An independent consultant project manager is primarily brought in to fill a role that the contracting organization cannot fill. This may be because the firm does not have any project managers to spare, does not have qualified project managers for that specific project, or—at some level—does not believe in the practice of project management. For whatever reason, the independent consultant project manager has a tremendous opportunity to create a very positive perception of project management and project managers within the client organization by representing the profession in a positive light. The project manager also has the chance to potentially choose which methodology and tools are most appropriate to the project—somewhat different than most of the other project manager career models mentioned above. This opportunity to have this type of input is often viewed as a very attractive advantage.

The major disadvantage of the independent consultant project manager role is uncertainty. The independent consultant project manager is only certain of being employed for the length of the current project. That can be three months, six months, a year…and after that, the consultant must find new work. This can be a very scary career model for many people—especially in post-2008 economic conditions. This process is often helped by contracting or staff augmentation firms that keep looking to identify opportunities for independent consultant project managers, as these companies only prosper when they find work for their consultants.

A quick note on staff augmentation firms: staff augmentation firms find work for independent consultant project managers through contacts they have at financial institutions and by subscribing to job posting services from these firms. These augmentation companies match the immediate needs of the institutions with the skill sets of project managers that they have identified through recruiting and networking, and connect the two. For this service, and sometimes for the service of processing payroll, these companies make a percentage of the money billed by the project manager.

Even with the help of staffing firms, it can be difficult to identify new projects quickly—especially if you have to continue to work full-time on your current assignment. Inherent in the independent consultant project manager process also comes the requirement of having to interview for new positions almost constantly. This, too, is seen by many as something of a "turn-off" as they consider becoming a consultant. An independent consultant project manager always needs to have a resume updated and ready to deliver, and be available to interview at a moment's notice. Also, the project manager might also have a travel component to their role, which may or may not be viewed as an attractive component to the job. Choosing the independent consultant project manager path in financial services is not for everyone, but it can be very rewarding.

An additional career path for project managers in the financial services space is that of technology vendor project manager. These are project managers whose major responsibly is to lead the implementation of technology (usually software) at client sites. As discussed in a previous chapter, this role is very different from the others in terms of expectations of skillset and experience. Still, it is a viable project manager career path within financial service with very distinct advantages and disadvantages.

As a whole, the advantages of following the technology vendor career path are a combination of those in the corporate project manager and firm-based consultant roles (Technology vendor project managers are, in fact, consultants). The projects in themselves are usually challenging, of good size and complexity, and are mostly staffed by very well-trained and motivated team members. Professional development opportunities are often present with the organization for which you work, as the improvement of the skills of a firm's consultants only improve the reputation and skills of the firm itself. Many of the professional safety factors are also present, as technology vendor project managers are primarily full-time employees, and not subject to the independent consultant project manager's practice of having to find and secure new projects without help. Financially, technology vendor project managers are normally compensated at a higher salary, as they often have a travel component, and, like firm-based and independent consultant project managers, are expected to have very specific talents in the area of client-facing consulting skills.

The specifics and content of the projects executed, however, can be viewed as the "downside" of being a technology vendor project manager. For the most part, a technology vendor project manager will be working on the same type (or very nearly the same type) of project every time. Whether working in software or hardware implementation, the technology vendor project manager is employed by a vendor with a specific set of products, and implementing and supporting those products is very clearly what the project manager will be working on. This can become somewhat monotonous if one is not completely enamored with the product set. In addition, there most likely will not be a tremendous opportunity to enhance the project management methods, processes, and toolsets of the firm with new ideas—odds are that the methodology to implement the firm's software or hardware has been around for a while, and though it may be dull, it is battle-tested. Travel can also become an issue, as a certain amount is often required of the technology vendor project manager. Another potential disadvantage to this and other project manager consulting roles is that a technology vendor project manager will sometimes be asked to assume the role of a business analyst. This happens often on projects where clients have not been convinced of the need for a paid project manager on their project. The same resource is therefore sold as, or evolves into, a part-time project manager/part-time business analyst. Project management viewpoints and philosophy aside, the technology vendor project manager has to be comfortable with playing that dual role, as well as be comfortable with the fact that our field of project management will always be undervalued as a technology vendor project manager. Stakeholder allegiances are fairly straightforward here, as the direct employer of the technology vendor project manager should be prioritized as the driver for most important project guidance. This might change should that vendor not perform ethically. Still, the role of technology vendor project manager is one viable choice for a career in financial services project management, as long as the prospective project manager knows the pros and cons.

One additional component deserving serious consideration when planning one's financial services project management career is the importance of obtaining a project management certification. In a recent sampling, out of thirteen advertisements for project manager jobs posted on CIO.com and Dice.com, eight ads either required or preferred project management certification. All eight ads are for mid- to senior-level IT project management positions that require anywhere from a minimum of five to eleven or more years of experience. Five of the eight ads say that project management certification is "highly desirable," "an advantage," "preferred," or "a plus." The three ads that require certification all specify the Project Management Institute's (PMI) Project Management Professional (PMP) credential.[59]

More and more CIOs believe in the importance of project management certifications, according to research from The Standish Group. The publisher of the CHAOS reports which track IT project success and failure rates says that two-thirds of CIOs it surveyed regard a PMI certification as valuable. The number of CIOs who require their project managers to be certified grew from 21 percent in 2005 to 31 percent by 2009.[60]

There are, of course, many different project management certifications, each having a slightly (or larger) different knowledgebase, acquisition process, and accep-

---

[59] Meridith Levinson, "Why Project Management Certifications Matter." January 20, 2010, CIO Magazine, http://www.cio.com/article/519213/Why_Project_Management_Certifications_Matter

[60] Ibid.

tance rate in the financial services industry. Here is a fairly comprehensive list, organized by issuing body:[61]

- Project Management Institute (PMI):
  - CAPM® (Certified Associate in Project Management)—An entry-level
    certification, designed for project team members and entry-level project
    managers.
  - PMP® (Project Management Professional)—One of the most widely-
    recognized PM credentials, this requires the demonstration of a solid
    foundation of project management knowledge and practice.
  - PgMP™ (Program Management Professional)—This certification is geared
    toward those who manage multiple projects.
  - PMI-RMP (PMI Risk Management Professional)—This certification is
    designed for individuals who advise and make project decisions based
    upon risk factors.
  - PMI-SP (PMI Scheduling Professional)—Certification in project
    management scheduling.
  - PMI-ACP (PMI Agile Certified Practitioner)—The newest PMI
    certification in Agile techniques.

- Scrum Alliance[62]
  - CSM (Certified Scrum Master)—Training in the Scrum fundamentals for
    ScrumMasters or Scrum team members.
  - CSPO (Certified Scrum Product Owner)—Basics of Scrum from the
    product owner's perspective. Training in managing a product backlog and
    working with a Scrum team.
  - CSP (Certified Scrum Professional)—Demonstrated experience,
    documented training, and proven knowledge in the art of Scrum.

- American Academy of Project Managers - The American Academy of Project
  Managers has several degrees, each requiring a high level of experience as well
  as graduate degrees, which are targeted toward executives and managers. These
  are "awarded" certifications, based on a review of a person's experience and
  credentials):

---

[61] Nicky LaMarco, "Types of PM Certifications," edited by Marlene Gundlach. Updated 8/30/2009;
http://www.brighthub.com/office/project-management/articles/47484.aspx
[62] http://www.scrumalliance.org/pages/scrum_certification

- o PME™ (Project Manager E-Business)
- o CIPM™ (Certified International Project Manager)
- o MPM™ (Master Project Manager)

- International Project Management Certifications
  - o Prince2—This certification is used extensively in the UK, both by the government and businesses. It is based on an examination process.
  - o Australian Institute of Project Management—Several levels of certifications geared primarily toward Australian project management professionals, based on international best practices.
  - o International Project Management Association—A Swiss organization, primarily geared toward national project management associations worldwide, has the longest history in the project management field.

So which is of most value professionally and/or financially to the financial services project manager? Experience had shown that the PMP certification is easily the most widely recognized certification in the industry, and the qualification most mentioned when the subject arises. Before the financial crisis of 2008 and the subsequent cuts to financial firms' training budgets, several large U.S. organizations were requiring that all staff who held the title of project manager be PMP certified. These companies would not only pay the cost of the exam, but often pay for any preparation classes or materials, and even pay the project manager's PMI membership dues. This practice has somewhat waned, but, by far, in all areas of financial services project management, the PMP certification gets you "more bang for the buck."

Beyond the PMP, Agile Scrum Master certification is also becoming more popular as the practice of Agile methods grows. More and more organizations are starting up pockets of Agile development initiatives, and hiring trained and certified resources is the quickest way to do so. The Agile certification is probably most desired by consulting and staff augmentation firms. Many full-service financial services firms— either hesitant to build their own internal Agile skill set or in a hurry to execute Agile projects—will turn to these professional services companies to supply them with consultants that they know are properly trained. Having the Agile Scrum certification proves to these organizations that the project manager has specifically chosen that skill and demonstrated some proficiency.

What about the financial benefits of having a project management certification? *There is both qualitative and quantitative evidence that having a recognized project management certification does improve a project manager's earning potential.* As mentioned above, more and more career opportunities—whether advertised or networked—require or strongly prefer a certification. Quantitatively, the PMI 2011 salary survey clearly shows that certified (in this case PMP certified) earn a higher salary.[63]

Annualized Salary by PMP Status

Status	n=	Percent	25th Percentile	Median	75th Percentile	Mean
Have a PMP Certification	10.668	79%	90,0000	107,000	128,232	111,824
PMP for less than 1 year	205	2%	80,000	95,400	113,000	99,237
PMP for 1 to less than 5 years	6,394	60%	86,000	102,500	123,000	107,304
PMP for 5 to less than 10 years	3,307	31%	97,000	113,000	135,000	118,625
PMP for 10 to less than 20 years	717	7%	100,000	120,000	140,000	124,610
PMP for 20 or more years	11	*	100,000	102,000	135,000	117,205
Do not have a PMP Certification	2,904	21%	74,500	92,465	115,000	97,829

Project Management Salary Survey, Seventh Addition, Project Management Institute 2011

There remains a very vibrant and exciting market in the financial services space for project managers. It is therefore up to us to understand the different paths down which we might drive our career, and the distinct pluses and minuses of each project manager career choice. Whether a project manager wants to work for a large corporation, be a consultant, or implement enterprise hardware or software, the roles associated with each can be challenging, but also hold very specific traits that should be understood up front before the choice is made. In this way, the project manager will make an educated decision, and choose the project manager road to professional and financial success.

---

[63] Project Management Salary Survey, Seventh Edition, Project Management Institute 2011

TIP: A PM Career in Financial Services is About Choice

As one considers a long-term career in financial services project management, the single most important characteristic that will become evident is the incredible number of choices one will have to consider. This can be a good or a bad thing. Having to choose a concentration, much like choosing a major in college, can be a very difficult process, as people have many unique and individual interests and wish to work on different things. What makes the sector a little more unique amongst its peers is that, with some exceptions (of course), the majority of financial services areas are great consumers of project management. The questions become: how and where do I work as a financial services project manager? What are my options?

There are, as mentioned, many.

Take, for example, the number of industry sectors that make up financial services. There are banks (numerous types such as commercial, retail, investment), and securities firms that buy, sell, and process the hundreds of millions of dollars traded in the global equity, bond, commodity, and currency markets. Then there are the insurance companies—mutual, life and casualty, commercial. There are other sectors as well, but the message here is that there is tremendous opportunity to choose one or several areas of professional focus within the financial domain, and be fairly comfortable in the fact the rewarding professional opportunities will be resident.

The types of opportunities—either in terms of the kinds of projects or the project management roles required—will also continue to offer choice and challenge. Technology-based projects will continue to be the mainstay of our industry, but even there the choices are many. Projects focused on systems integration, full-lifecycle software development, conversions, selections, and implementations all will be plentiful in financial services over the coming years.

Choice will also remain in the types of roles available to PMs in financial services. Large institutions will continue to hire full-time project managers to deliver internal projects, and also look to engage both independent contractors as well as full-service consulting firms to help them in areas where internal resources are inexperienced not available. Product vendors also will be looking for qualified PMs to assist them in implementing enterprise applications, such as trading and portfolio management systems or enterprise resource management (ERP) platforms.

With all of this choice comes a bit of confusion. A PM in financial services must first begin to understand—at a fairly detailed level—the foundational elements of the area of interest. This is not always easy, as industry overview training is usually delivered once one *has* a job. The tip here is to do your research—online or in person at industry events—and jump right in. You may have an idea that consulting is your dream job, only to find later on that you enjoy the comfort and camaraderie of a large corporation. The good news is, if you are a project manager in financial services, you have a choice.

CHAPTER 15:
The Use of Project Management Tools in Financial Services

Thomas Carlyle, a famous historian and author, stated, "Man is a tool-using animal. Without tools he is nothing, with tools he is all."[64] Financial services project managers are tool-using animals as well. And, as has been the trend, they are animals inconsistent in the tools they use and the means in which they use them.

There are many areas in which tools can be utilized to assist in the overall project management process. It is not only Microsoft Project that is the be-all and end-all—throughout the project lifecycle, specific software and manual process assistors are available to make project delivery more efficient. Tools can be techniques for identifying requirements, evaluating potential technology vendors, or delivering communications, but tools are primarily used to manage financial services projects in the areas of *schedule management* and *time and cost management.* There are also software applications that look to combine these processes (and more) into *project portfolio management (PPM)* toolsets.

Schedule management focus primarily on planning and tracking the progress of project-related activities based on dependencies, resources, and actual results. The most common project schedule management tool in financial services—and other industries—is *Microsoft Project.* Depending on your source, *Microsoft Project* is estimated to hold +/- 90 percent of the market for project scheduling software applications. It

---

[64] www.augsburg.edu/ppages/~schwalbe

is not the only one—but it is the biggest. Whether using MS Project, a competitor, or s simple Excel (Microsoft again!) spreadsheet, every project in financial services looks to some tool to track a projects schedule. How this tracking is done, and for what reasons, vary greatly across the industry. It is very common in financial organizations with somewhat immature project management processes to compose a project schedule using high-level activities, assign an end date based on a real or perceived business objective, type this information into a MS PowerPoint slide, and consider themselves now more than ready to begin the schedule management process. As mentioned above, Excel is also used quite frequently to compose a simple list of project activities, document the dates on which the project manager envisions their delivery, maybe add a "comments" column, and that becomes the project schedule. The downside (among many) of the two methods mentioned above is that, in those two applications, there is really no way to identify or track the dependencies between the activities, and therefore *no way to assess the impact of a change* to any of the dates. There is also no way to track progress—except for inserting a table column named "progress" and typing in an "guestimated" percent complete (which is, sadly, the method many very senior project managers use on very complex scheduling applications). The upside to using applications such as PowerPoint or Excel is their obvious familiarity to the stakeholder community at large; because of this, the documents produced are easily communicated through email and collaboration software and available to read or edit on almost any desktop. In this case, however, this author must weigh in and state very sternly: "Please, ***NO PROJECT MANAGEMENT BY POWERPOINT!***" Reasons why are below in the *Tips* box.

Project scheduling management software is very popular in the financial services industry; applications such as Microsoft Project, Primavera P6, and @task are very common on the desktops of industry project managers, with MS Project being the most popular. These are what are termed in the market "mid-tier" applications—more robust than simple MS Office applications like Excel and Word, but as not big as some EPM or PPM tools (more on those later). Although organizations fairly consistently possess these "mid-tier" applications, the way they are used in our industry varies greatly.

In simplest terms, project scheduling applications can be used to estimate and track both effort and duration. *For most projects in the financial services industry, schedule management means duration management.* Duration, as we remember from a previous chapter, is the length of time from the start of an activity to the estimated end of the activity. The duration of the activity can be affected by the number of resources assigned to the task, their availability, and their level of expertise. Durations of activities can also be affected by any other tasks identified as predecessors or successors. Most scheduling software allows you to manipulate these variables to get realistic duration estimates. Unfortunately, financial firms often do not use this functionality, and view duration purely as how long a task will take no matter what. What this means is that *the project manager will set the length of time an activity is expected to take, then assume that no matter who works on it during that time, or how many hours, or who they may get to help—none of this will affect the duration.* Though this appears somewhat short-sighted, project managers in our industry do this for several reasons. The first reason is that this is the simplest and easiest way to communicate the progress of a project. Although factoring in effort and expertise may give one a more accurate picture, the time it takes to both accurately process and, more importantly, *explain* to one's stakeholders the intricacies of one's estimating model may outweigh the value that it adds. Secondly, it can be *very difficult* to accurately represent the effect of resources and dependencies on a project schedule. This is because of the widespread use of a shared services model for project work in our industry. Because it is most likely that the resources assigned to your project are also assigned to many more, accurately estimating their participation on a project at the task level can be next to impossible. The final reason for using scheduling software purely at the duration level is probably the simplest—it's really too hard to use it any other way. The manual processing required to accurately estimate and track individual resources at the task level often requires more time and training than the project manager has available.

Time and cost management tools are those that assist the project manager in estimating and tracking the actual effort and associated cost it will take to complete a project. This functionality can either be found integrated into other project applications—such as MS Project—or standing alone. Time and cost management tools are less often creative utilizations of current spreadsheets (though MS Excel has a timesheet application), and more often fully functional systems designed to accurately capture project effort. Home-grown solutions exist, too, as many financial institutions, unhappy with the commercially available options, have decide to develop and support their own time management systems.

From a functional perspective, time management tools simply modernize the legacy paper timesheet. The applications assign estimated effort to a project resource, then look to capture how much of that effort is exerted during the project against a specific activity or deliverable. Most often, that effort is then associated with a cost, giving the project manager a measurement of how much time and cost have been expended on the project.

There are literally dozens of time and cost management systems available commercially. Many are targeted at professional services firms that need to track the time spent by their consultants on projects so that they can effectively bill their clients. Time and cost management systems are also used by larger banks and institutions to help their internal organizations understand the true effort and cost associated with completing their own projects.

One unique aspect of the use of time and cost management systems in financial services is that, for the majority of projects found outside the professional services sector, *there is rarely a connection between the time and cost management system and the schedule management system.* This is true when both are present, and even when the schedule or time management system contains functionality to accomplish the other metric—for example, MS Project has time- and cost-tracking capabilities, but companies often use standalone or internally developed time sheet systems on the same projects being scheduled in MS Project. This bifurcated process increases the difficulty of tracking true project progress, and often skews the stakeholders' perception of the project (I can't be over budget—I'm behind schedule!)

Project portfolio management is the management of the IT projects undertaken to maximize the contribution of business value of projects to the company.[65] It is not the management of individual projects, but an overall strategy of choosing and continually evaluating the combination of right projects to execute against a company's strategy. The mature existence of this direct alignment between project delivery and corporate vision is uncommon in the financial services space, and often becomes the "holy grail" of corporate initiatives. Most firms are set up to identify and execute projects that—in the best case—benefit their own small circle of influence (internal stakeholders and direct customers). A process for evaluating, prioritizing, and delivering a combination of projects organizationally decreed as strategic (and then managing them in a synergistic manner) will most likely be foreign. The implementation of a project portfolio management process within a financial services firm is, therefore, often driven by recommendations developed by external consultants, and often involves the implementation of PPM tools.

PPM tools, by definition, are more robust in their functionality than standard project scheduling or time management systems because of the scope of the organization and complexity of project data these systems must manage. The project manager will be using these systems not only to set up and manage Gantt charts and budgets, but as a strategic tool to acquire real-time data on the health of the corporate future. Therefore, PPM functionality normally includes project alignment, risk assessment,

---

[65] http://www.cioupdate.com/trends/article.php/3505701/Making-Sense-of-PProject Manager-Software.htm

demand forecasting, portfolio analysis and reporting, resource management, financial analysis, "what-if" analysis, benefits measurement, and incorporation of the standard project management disciplines (like scheduling, timing, tracking, and budget management).[66]

PPM tools can have a dramatic impact on the delivery of projects. According to a 2008 IDC study, organizations had huge cost savings when they implemented a PPM solution:

- Cost per project fell by 37 percent.
- Redundant projects dropped by 78 percent.
- Project failure rates decreased by 59 percent.
- Time-to-market for revenue generating initiatives dropped by 33 percent.

In a Gantry Group study, key findings included "savings of 6.5 percent of the average annual budget by the end of year one, and 14 percent (NPV) over a three-year deployment period." PPM software helped organizations:

- Improve the annual average for project timeliness by 45.2 percent.
- Reduce management time spent on project status reporting by 43.2 percent, reclaiming 3.8 hours of each manager's workweek.
- Reduce management time spent on labor capitalization report by 54.7 percent, recouping 3.6 hours per report.
- Decrease the time to achieve financial sign-off for new projects by 20.4 percent, or 8.4 days.

Many financial services organizations attempt to implement PPM tools, with mixed results. Cultural hurdles are one reason, as the implementation of such a strategy would force internal organizations to be more transparent with their peers in regards to financial and performance information. PPM tools also have a difficult time in any organization that has not instituted organizational standards for project, HR, and financial management. In order for a system or process to work across a whole firm, the way performance is measured across that firm must be standardized. The overall project lifecycle has to be disciplined as well. Project portfolio management not only decides what projects to start, but also keeps track of them through their lifecycle, evaluates their performance, and makes changes (including cancelling projects) as time moves along. The delivering organization has to have in place the process and

---

[66] http://www.cioupdate.com/trends/article.php/3505701/Making-Sense-of-PProject Manager-Software.htm

discipline to accurately manage their projects from initiation to closure, and have in place the organizational metrics mentioned above.

Project portfolio management is usually a major component of what has been observed in many financial services organizations as a drive to the promised land—*Project Management Nirvana*. In Project Management Nirvana, the entire organization understands the firm's corporate strategy, and will only plan on projects that support that vision. Nirvana includes an automated process (demand management) that initiates a project request, then routes that request—complete with estimates on all of the project evaluation measures—to a system and governing body that evaluates all requests based on the agreed upon organizational assessment criteria and chooses the initiatives based on their merit and alignment with corporate strategy. Once the project receives initial approval, it is sent through the workflow system to the Enterprise Resource Planning (ERP) System where the staffing database is searched for the preliminary resource requirements outlined in the project request. These resources will be selected based on matching skillsets, level of experience, and availability—all this residing in the ERP system. An available and properly qualified project manager will be assigned at this point as well. This project manager will take this project request and initial resource plan and be systematically guided to the organization's knowledge management library, where the manager can view historical project results that may be similar to this project, then use that, or any of the scores of project plan templates, methods, and deliverables, to begin the initial estimation process. Calling on appropriate all available resources, the project manager "fleshes out" the project plan until it is an agreed-upon estimate of effort, duration, and cost. Once signed off by the team and sponsor, this initial estimate will be loaded into the organization's PPM system, where team members can view their assigned tasks, access training aids and other useful information to help them execute the project, track their time, view project status, and communicate with the project manager and other team members. The project manager, in turn, can communicate with all the stakeholders, request status from team members, approve time, manage risks and issues logs, and overall manage the project on a tactical level. Financial information from the project is captured and reported in "real time" to sponsor, stakeholders, and management through the PPM system, as is progress against the project plan. This in turn is used to make decisions on any change in direction or funding requirements that may evolve. Once the project has been successfully completed, the results of the project are loaded into the knowledge management library for the next project manager to use.

Sound too good to be true? In truth, all of the above is possible. Unfortunately, it never comes together as well as represented in the example. Organizations are sometimes successful in implementing pieces of this framework, but connecting all the dots usually takes a discipline and dedication that few organizations can deliver. Most often, PPM solutions have had a hard time reconciling robust functionality and the needs of the varied user groups responsible for their implementation and support. Applications like Primavera, Artemis, Plainview, and MS Project Enterprise Server have long been the domain of specialists. Companies that tried integrating this kind of software throughout the organization have encountered long and costly training sessions with significant interruption in people's workflow. More often than not, the software ends up only being used by a small group of project management specialists and is something of a burden on everyone else.[67]

The bottom line in understanding the use of project management tools may lie less in "*Man is a tool-using animal. Without tools he is nothing,*" and more in "*A fool with a tool is still a fool.*" The successful use of any tools in financial services project management, be it an enterprise PPM application or a simple set of macros in Excel, depends on the understanding of the project management process and its required discipline. Tools can improve an already strong process, but worsen one that is inefficient or significantly flawed.

---

[67] http://www.vertabase.com/blog/2-key-features-of-enterprise-project-management-software/

> ### TIP: *"No Project Management by PowerPoint!"*
>
> How many times have we been asked to just put together a "high-level timeline" slide for an executive presentation only to find out that the manager has somehow affected the space-time continuum with his magic scheduling mouse to now deliver the project six months early? A click here, some Smart Art there and… voila! Four weeks of planning your carefully sequenced and resourced activities has become a big blue diamond labeled "Phase 2—TBD." Slide the mouse to the left and…poof! You've cut a year from your schedule!
>
> Now, as project managers we all are aware of the need for summary information. And we also know that a lot of people do not feel comfortable presenting information with such tools as MS Project. Still, we need to explain to our stakeholders that just because you can contract the size of a rectangular "timeline" on a PowerPoint slide does not mean that the laws of physics are sidestepped—and work that usually takes 40 hours now takes 40 minutes. Maybe if you make them go back and actually see if the schedule can possibly be made to look like the pretty picture, then they'd be a little less cavalier with the clip art.

CHAPTER 16:
The Future of Project Management in the Financial Services Industry

So what does the future hold for project management (and project managers!) in the financial services industry? Are there breakthrough technologies, processes, or ideas that will suddenly innovate the way we manage projects? Will there be sweeping changes in the financial markets—be they regulatory, economic, or cultural—that will have an impact on the idea of projects and project management?

One way to begin to answer these questions is to look at some of the current or emerging trends in project management and in the industry and examine their future. One of the hottest trends right now is the concept of Agile project management. As mentioned in a previous chapter, the concept of Agile project management is based on individuals and interactions over processes and tools, working software over comprehensive documentation, customer collaboration over contract negotiation, and responding to change over following a plan.[68] The Agile approach has become extremely popular as a "trendy" methodology if an organization wishes to portray an image of being current and nimble—unlike the old stodgy financial institutions of

---

[68] Manifesto for Agile Software Development, 2001, Kent Beck, Mike Beedle, Arie van Bennekum, Alistair Cockburn, Ward Cunningham, Martin Fowler, James Grenning, Jim Highsmith, Andrew Hunt, Ron Jeffries, Jon Kern, Brian Marick, Robert C. Martin, Steve Mellor, Ken Schwaber, Jeff Sutherland, Dave Thomas

the past. Agile has its own professional development track[69]—CSM (Certified Scrum Master), CSPO (Certified Scrum Product Owner)—and appears as at least a preferred skillset in many career employment opportunity ads. But what is the future of Agile in financial services?

This author continues to predict that *Agile as a project approach will remain challenged to significantly penetrate the larger financial institutions.* The overriding culture of financial organizations—the need for extreme measures of auditability, of fear-based protection of information, of pursuing mandates versus innovation—lies in the direct path of wider Agile adoption. In addition, heavily regulated industries—like financial services—often legally require the level of added administration and documentation that Agile attempts to minimize. It is this combination of cultural and practical circumstances that make Agile's future in our industry cloudy. That is not to say that the philosophical concepts of Agile "thinking" cannot be applied. There are thought-leaders in our industry directing organizations to explore different methods of project and product management. One such consulting firm—Emergn, Ltd.—says that one of the effects of introducing thinking around agility into the IT development process is that it encourages greater questioning about how development programs should be actioned. They propose that many organizations are realizing that identifying the right sets of practices for their specific environment has greater value than making blanket assumptions about adopting a single approach—a mistake made by many about Agile early on. Even a paper produced by ESI[70] highlighting their predictions for the top ten trends in project management identifies a more blended approach as the future of Agile.

The future may also see a tighter connection between project management and business process management. This will be particularly prevalent in our financial services industry, where there always has been a drive to continually reduce the costs of processing. An associated trend here will be a wider use of business process management methodologies—such as Lean. Large organizations, such as State Street Corporation in Boston, are starting to build much of their strategic project approach around Lean methods.

Project teams that are distributed globally will continue to become more the norm, challenging both our human and technological resources. No longer will there simply be "offshoring," but fully functional workgroups will be essential to delivering

---

[69] http://www.scrumalliance.org/pages/scrum_certification

[70] ESI Announces Top 10 Project Management Trends for 2012, http://www.esi-intl.com/~/media/Files/Public-Site/US/Newsroom/NewsReleases2012/PM-Trends-2012.ashx

in the truly global environment in which we now work. Cultural boundaries will now be stretched, as our project reject teams will have to learn not just how to communicate, but how to collaborate across cultures.

Trending also will be the importance of client value versus the triple constraints. *Project managers will become more responsible for the value their product brings to the client than for being on schedule or under budget.* A project may still be deemed a success if it is late and costs more than expected, as long as it meets or exceeds the expected value of the product recipient.

Some of the other future trends in project management identified by ESI include:

- Program management will gain momentum, but resources will remain in short supply.
- Collaboration software solutions will become an essential business tool for project teams.
- "Learning transfer" will become the new mantra, but with little structured application.
- Internal certifications in corporations and federal agencies will eclipse the PMP®.
- More PMO heads will measure effectiveness on business results.
- Good project managers will buck unemployment trends.
- HR professionals will seek assessments to identify high-potential project managers.

From a financial services industry perspective, the future promises to bring change—change in how the industry looks at customers, at technology, and at their businesses as a whole. Recently, a report put out by Intuit highlights four key industry future trends and their impacts[71]

1. ***There will be a new playing field for financial services***—Nontraditional competitors using new technology, business models, and in some cases regulatory advantages will target attractive market segments. Scale and regulatory-driven industry consolidation will require most financial institutions to decide whether to stay independent, be acquired, or become an acquirer. Strategic partnering will increase, both as a way to gain scale and as an alternative to consolidation, and industry change will create growth opportunities. Financial institutions that don't adapt are at risk of being relegated to highly regulated, low-margin and -growth providers of commodity services.

---

[71] Intuit 2020. *The Future of Financial Services* http://www.banking2020.com/wp-content/uploads/2011/04/intuit_corp_banking2020_0311-FINAL.pdf

2. *Customer segments will shift, and markets will change*—Efficiency and profitability require virtual service and support excellence; personal service will still be necessary to maintain strong customer relationships. The risk shift creates new opportunities for financial institutions to become trusted advisors and provide a range of fee-based services. Women are increasingly responsible for financial decisions; banks that understand their needs will be able to develop strong, profitable relationships with them.

3. *Financial services organizations will accelerate their use of technology to meet customer needs*—The rise of tablets, smartphones, and apps will create new opportunities for financial institutions to improve customer service, cut costs, and create new fee-based products and services. The proliferation and demand for mobile devices provide customers with access to their financial institutions anytime and anywhere, and financial institutions that can effectively unlock the value of data to deliver valuable insights to customers will gain significant operational and competitive advantages.

4. *Over the next decade, the financial service industry will shift its focus from transactions to customized value-added services*—The role of financial institutions will change from "owning" the primary relationship secured by loans and deposits to being part of a team of expert service providers, with the customer deciding who owns the primary relationship. Financial institutions will actively build and manage their social reputations by active participation in on and offline social activities. Community-based financial institutions will build upon their local knowledge and connections to create trusted relationships with influential business and community leaders.

In the securities industry, firms will look to both globalize and localize to boost revenues and cut costs. Over the next three to five years, large securities firms will face an imperative to tap into fast-growing markets to boost revenue, while simultaneously offshoring IT, business processes and other functions to reduce costs. Technology will also be a focus, as organizations focus on adapting technology to improve service delivery. Securities firms will strengthen their ties with customers by using technology and innovation to provide better service and delivery. Increased compliance effectiveness will also be a focus, as expanding regulations, overlapping mandates, and tighter enforcement worldwide continue to raise the cost of compliance and increase the consequences of noncompliance. Enhanced risk management will be key—securities firm executives have become increasingly aware that reputational problems can irreparably damage their business, yet they feel it is the most difficult risk to manage.

One additional future imperative will be the ability to adapt to an aging population. As a result of declining birth rates and longer life expectancy, wealthy countries will increasingly have more old people and fewer young. In addition, as the baby boomers retire, the ranks of the middle-aged will also dwindle. Between 2000 and 2050, the percentage of America's population over the age of sixty-five will grow from 12 percent to 21 percent, while the share of the population aged forty to sixty-four will fall from a peak of 33 percent in 2010 to 28 percent by 2040. In Japan and some European countries, the shift will be even more dramatic.[72]

So what does the future hold for project management in financial services? First off, *although collaborative methodologies like Agile will continue to find pockets of acceptance, the "meat and potatoes" of project management methods—especially from IT-related projects—will be Waterfall.* This will be the mainstay, as the wider acceptance of other approaches will continue to be hindered by the risk-averse culture of financial services firms and the predicted growth in both internal and regulation and governance.

Financial services project managers will assume more business and financial responsibility for their projects and the results of their projects, but may not immediately have the tools to deliver. This is because assigning project managers to be accountable will not necessarily speed up adoption of improvement of their time and cost management systems. As discussed, the effectiveness of the tools that financial project managers use varies greatly, and it is often difficult to find an integrated process that accurately manages *both* time and cost. Until the growing number of PPM tools can be effectively utilized, the true effectiveness of business project management will continue to lag.

The financial service industry will continue to be a growth market in terms of project management employment. With the projected growth in IT spending over the next five to ten years moving to the $500 billion mark, the initiation of significant new regulation, and the constant need for new products and services, our industry will always need project managers. What may also grow is the number of project manager service providers, as the market for project manager training and consulting continues to grow.

Financial institutions will more aggressively pursue PPM strategies, but be challenged to "onboard" strong talent and acceptable systems. The importance of managing a company's projects as a portfolio of complementary initiatives each contributing to the overall company strategy will continue to become more important to financial institutions. Unfortunately, the skills to effectively manage a *program*—not a project—are

---

[72] Deloitte Touche Tohmatsu, Global Securities Industry Outlook, Jeff Kottkamp, National Securities Leader, Deloitte & Touche USA LLP

very difficult to find in an employee. Most project managers are trained as such, and require additional education and experience to manage a program. Even more difficult to find is an easily implemented and accepted PPM system to support the program. As mentioned, many very good systems do exist, but getting an organization to utilize them is extremely difficult. Often the robust functionality that is necessary to manage the program is only ever really used by the program managers or the occasional "power user." Otherwise, many less project management-savvy team members will see the PPM tool as overhead and a nuisance, and never use it.

The future for project management and project managers in the financial services sector remains bright. There appears to be growth in available and rewarding employment, and there are often opportunities for significant professional development. The various employment methods—full-time, firm-base, independent consultant—will remain and grow. The danger lies in the potential risk of another financial crisis or an influx of regulations so broad-based that the industry needs to rethink itself as a whole. Absent that event, project management in financial services remains a place where a project manager can find financial, personal, and professional success. Given the future, it's a good place to be.

ABOUT THE AUTHOR

Todd Loeb is a successful consultant, speaker, author, and blogger in the areas of project management tactics and strategy, communications and soft skills, and staff recruiting and development. He has over twenty-five years of front-line project management, leadership, and technology experience in the financial services industry.

During the last twenty-five years, Todd has worked with such organizations as State Street Corporation, Bank of New York/Mellon, Thomson Financial, Barclay's, and Liberty Mutual Insurance. He has managed the design, development, and implementation of several multi-million dollar technology platforms, as well as assisted multiple clients in dramatically improving their internal project management practices. Todd is President and The Mascar Group, created in 2007.

The Mascar Group is a financial services project management knowledge center that delivers strategic and tactical assistance in the improvement of project execution through hands-on consulting, group presentations, and the publication of new ideas. Services include:

- Staffing of projects
- Public speaking—large or small groups
- Book publishing
- Blog
- Primary research
- Other media—Twitter, Facebook, LinkedIn, podcast

Todd is a member of PMI and has been a certified Project Management Professional (PMP) since 2003.

For information about the services and products of The Mascar Group, please visit the company's website at www.mascargroup.com or send an email to toddloeb@mascargroup.com.

19092108R00093

Made in the USA
Middletown, DE
03 April 2015